The Missionary Adventures
of
Bob & Arty

Volume 6

The Case of the
Skeptic Doctor

by Jeff Barth

The
Missionary Adventures
of
Bob & Arty
series

Volume 6

The Case of the
Skeptic Doctor

Copyright 2017
by Jeff Barth

ISBN - 978-1-891484-05-6

Contents

Chapter	Page
1 A Family Picnic	1
2 A Creation Bible Study	13
3 Diner Discussion	25
4 A Call to Action	39
5 Off to the Amazon	53
6 Over the Big Pond	67
7 Heavy Devastation	83
8 A Daring Parachute Rescue	99
9 Through the Swamp	119
10 Journey Up the River	135
11 Reunion	151
12 The Skeptic's Quest	161
13 The Skeptic Wrestles	179
14 The Skeptic Surrenders	193

Old Gabe

Chapter 1

A Family Picnic

It was Sunday afternoon, and Bob and Arty Baxter were in the office of their missionary headquarters there in the air-truck freight terminal, owned and operated by their father Jesse Baxter, going through their weekly mail.

"How's a little hike up Mount Philo sound this afternoon? We could pack a little picnic supper and enjoy watching the sunset across Lake Champlain," Arty said glancing over to his brother's desk to get his reaction.

"Good idea, and I'm sure we could interest Josh and Christy and Bess and Dad and Mom to come along," Bob proposed.

The walk up Mount Philo in Charlotte

had become a favorite afternoon outing for the Baxter family ever since their first hike up the six-hundred-foot elevation of Mount Philo which was once a favorite sentinel post from centuries past used by the natives and settlers to survey the maritime travelers on Lake Champlain.

"Sounds fun...and you couldn't ask for better weather for the first of May," Bob said glancing at the thermometer in the window. "It says 70 degrees, and with this dry air it feels just right," he added turning his attention back to the letter he had in his hand. "Hey, Arty, this is an interesting letter from some sweet Christian widow lady from upper state New York across the lake."

"Yeah, what's it about?"

"This lady lost her doctor husband to a heart attack last winter, and she said one of his last requests of her, before he went on to be with the Lord, was if she would try again to reach out to his long estranged brother who was also a medical doctor and who had been doing some humanitarian medical work for years in South America. She says they had been trying to reach him by letters this winter after his brother's pass-

A Family Picnic

ing, but, in spite of trying to send at least a half a dozen letters to him over the winter, they were yet to hear back from him... and she was willing to give our ministry a rather large contribution if we would be willing to help her out in not only taking word to her brother-in-law about her husband's and his brother's untimely death...but also because both she and her deceased husband had always had concerns about the authenticity of her husband's brother's relationship with God... she wants us to fly down there and speak personally to him about this great need. She said her brother-in-law was a good man and self-sacrificing, but that she feared he might be trying to use his 'good works' to try to earn his way to heaven, and they want to reach out to him. Plus she knew that the supplies we could take down to him would be more than appreciated and would help a lot of needy natives with the vast flooding down there."

"There are other particulars that she relates in the letter," Bob commented and then continued, "and she wondered if we would want to take a short trip across Lake Champlain to Ticonderoga, NY, where she resides. She says that her late husband had conducted a Wednesday Bible Study in their home for years, and it had phased into a home church, and that they have several nice home schooling families attending their church that she was sure either we or our whole family would enjoy meeting. They have strong conservative values, she says, and meet on Sunday mornings...and if we could make it over some Sunday or Wednesday sometime she would like to give us an opportunity to share a little about our mission work with the group. One of the men in her group, who's an engineer, was doing some discussions on Creation for their Wednesday Bible Study, and she thought that might interest us as well."

"Hmm, does sound interesting," Arty agreed nodding. "Have to run it by Dad and see what he thinks."

"Anyway, it's a nice letter...maybe I could take it with me and share it over supper with the family up on top Mount Philo," Bob replied.

"Good...let's go and see what's going on at home," Arty said jumping up from his desk, and the two brothers were soon outside climb-

A Family Picnic

ing into their International Scout that was fondly donated to the ministry by their grandfather.

Heading down the back roads and turning up their long tree-lined driveway, Arty noticed grandma and grandpa out back of their house across the meadow, under the sugar maple swinging on their long bench swing. "Don't suppose Grama and Grampa would want to go do you?" Arty wondered.

"I'm sure they'd like to, but Gramps said Grama's back has been giving her fits lately, and so I don't think she'll be up for it ... that's a pretty rigorous hike even for Mom and Dad," Bob reminded his brother.

"Oh, sure, I didn't think of that," Arty said as he wheeled the Scout into its parking spot and turned off the engine.

In less than an hour the girls had thrown together a dinner of chili dogs and potato salad and carrot pennies and some cupcakes they had the night before, and the family was in the station wagon heading south to Mount Philo State Park.

There were lots of other folks using the afternoon for a healthy hike, and some had brought their dogs along to give them a chance to romp around. The road up the Mount was partly paved but then turned into gravel as they ascended the first straightaway and then a few big hairpin turns. The woods on both sides was densely populated with sugar maples which now were, of course, leafing out; but just a few weeks before this lower tier of the woods was a favorite maple sap sugaring run for the nearby farmer. A careful study of the bottom 5 feet of most of the trees revealed where a sap tap had been placed and were healing over where the tap holes had been drilled. Most of the trees were about a foot in diameter or better that had been tapped, but every once in a while they would come upon what the old timers called a "limber". These were huge old maple trees of a good four to six feet in girth, and up about 8 to 10 feet off the ground, there were big limbs of maybe 2 to 3 feet in diameter swinging out and up from the main trunk. Directly under these big limbs is where the experienced sugar maker put his tap, because he knows these taps so located will yield the most and often the sweetest sap; thus those big trees were called "limbers".

A Family Picnic

"Boy, look at that limber," Dad said pointing at the big maple standing alone just off the road. I'll bet they must have put 8 or 10 buckets on that tree," he added with a smile.

This set the boys to an immediate close investigation of the trunk as they headed for the tree, and soon one by one they located the spots where the taps had been drilled and counted exactly 8 sites. The girls looked to their father and smiling Christy said, "How'd you know there were that many?"

"Oh, I didn't know for sure...it was just a guess," Jesse smiled modestly.

The tree-lined road soon gave way to smaller and shorter trees and huge boulders some as big as a bus along the side of the trail, which brought a comment from Josh, "I'd say that bolder has been in that same spot since the flood?"

"Could be," added Bob, "as long as the receding ice from the Ice Age didn't move it along a little."

The hikers kept their steady pace, but Mom and Dad were obliged a few times to pause to catch their breath. And then the girls would

The Case of the Skeptic Doctor

take a few moments to admire the profusion of wildflowers that were on the forest floor that were taking advantage of the direct sun before the trees leafed out all the way putting the flowers in the shade. The intricate design of some of those flowers brought a comment from Bessy as they studied a tiny "jack in the pulpit" flower. "Solomon and all his glory wasn't arrayed like one of these!"

"Yep," added Josh admiring the flower, "it just shows you how unimpressive man in all his glorious works really is...God can make just a simple little wildflower more glorious than all that man can do."

With such observations and small talk the winded hikers at last made their way to the level road at the top of the summit where they came upon a ranger's station beside a large parking area with a couple of cars, vehicles of those explorers who felt their climb of Mt. Philo was better experienced with a little less physical exertion; although the road was free of guard rails, and at some spots there was a good 50 to 100 foot drop off, no doubt putting some of their passengers in their cars under a good bit of stress

A Family Picnic

anyway as they squirmed in there seats as they slowly squeezed around the turns.

Once across the parking lot it was a short walk out to the overlook area where there were some sturdy guard rails to lean against as the family gazed in awe at the amazing expanse of Lake Champlain laying dramatically below and in front of them from this famous lookout spot. They all stood and looked for a good while first at the distant Adirondack Mountains across Lake Champlain and then the farms below, watching the traffic progressing in the foreground like tiny toy cars and trucks going north and south on Route 7.

"Can you see Fort Ticondaroga from up here?" Bob asked.

"I don't think so," Arty replied gazing to the farther south regions of the lake.

"I don't see anything like a fort?" Josh declared turning the binocular televiewer that was there mounted on the rail post. Scanning the region for a few minutes at last the machine made a clanging sound, and the view shutters closed.

"It's going to take someone wealthier

The Case of the Skeptic Doctor

than me to continue this exploration... I just used my last quarter for the first 10 minutes," Josh said smiling looking to the others.

Arty was next and then Bob added a little humor, "Old Sam Champlain would have loved to have had one of these binocular viewers at his disposal when mapping out this lake."

At last the guys grew tired of their diversions, and growing hungry their sisters came and called them to dinner on the nearby picnic tables as the sun was dropping low in the western sky. Soon there would be a display of reddish golden beauty in the sky, and so they sat down for dinner so they could enjoy the sunset as they descended the mountain along the northwestern roadway that went down the backside of the mountain. While eating, Bob got out the letter from the widow lady and began to share its contents with his family.

After Bob had informed them of the letter's gist and giving them the widow lady's name, Jesse Baxter tilted his head as if he was trying to recall. "I think I remember meeting her husband...or maybe it was his brother way back at a pilot training course I taught over in

A Family Picnic

Plattsburgh. Do you fellas remember when we went over there about 10 years ago for that primitive landing class I gave for prospective missionaries? That was him," father declared at last remembering..."Dr. Wes Armstrong. He was a doctor interested in going to South America, and he had a young son with him...remember?"

"Oh, yeah, I remember," Bob replied. "He sat in the front row with his boy...his boy was about our age, wasn't he?"

"Yeah...he was the nicest guy... I wonder if it was her husband or her brother-in-law?" Jesse pondered, and then added, "Sounds like a good opportunity to meet some folks...maybe you and Arty should try going to their Bible Study sometime and check em out a little bit, before we all go."

"Okay, Dad," Bob replied, "we were just wanting to see how you felt about it... maybe we will go this Wednesday. Mrs. Armstrong says they meet for Bible Study every couple of weeks on Wednesday evenings, and it comes up this week...they have been doing a study conducted by one of the fathers on Creation, and that's always an interesting topic," Bob added.

The Case of the Skeptic Doctor

"Sounds good to me," their father replied looking to mother for her reaction, and she just smiled in agreement.

Soon the family was making their way down the gentle roadway watching the beautiful sky in the west light up with God's amazing handiwork rejoicing together.

Chapter 2

A Creation Bible Study

When Bob and Arty arrived at the home of the widow Mrs. Lydia Armstrong it was still light out for the seven o'clock meeting. The brothers were introduced to a few of the folks, but most of the mothers who had younger children stayed home, but there were a few teens with about 5 dads who were milling around on the front lawn and porch making small talk. Mrs. Armstrong was so kind and joyful and said she wanted the brothers to meet her 22 year old nephew Craig who just then was coming up the porch steps reaching out his hand for a shake. He was of a slender build, sandy hair and fairly nicely dressed and about their height.

The Case of the Skeptic Doctor

"Craig Armstrong," he said with a big smile, "glad to see you fellows again... I think we were all little guys the last time we met."

"Yeah, we were," Bob smiled, "and was that at that flight training seminar my dad gave up in Plattsburgh?"

"Yep, I think that was it, and my dad was just beginning to think about missions work at that time and was going to fly down to Brazil for some short term medical work with a group of volunteer doctors, and he was going to be flying out to the bush or jungle and needed some pointers on how to manage his Beechcraft airplane in those rugged conditions."

"How'd he do with it? Has he made a few trips down?" asked Arty

"Yeah, he goes down every year for several months, and I'm hoping to join him down there with his work after I get out of med school or maybe even sooner."

With seeing the young men taking to easy conversation Mrs. Armstrong smiled and went over to talk with a group of ladies.

Bob and Arty continued to talk with their renewed acquaintance as they gazed around at

A Creation Bible Study

the small crowd of maybe 15 people or so.

"Yeah, my aunt said she was thinking about hiring you fellas to fly down and visit my dad, and that sounded really cool... I wonder if it would be possible for me to tag along?"

"Well, sure," Bob replied glancing over to Arty who nodded in affirmative. "We really don't know much about the particulars yet, but we'll sure keep it in mind, but your aunt said you were in college right now."

"Yep, I'm a med student at UVM."

The fellas continued their small talk, but then one of the fathers beckoned the small crowd to find their way to the family room. A Mr. Ed Hamilton who was a civil engineer, and also did small group teaching on Creation science, was up front adjusting his overhead projector on the screen on the back wall trying his overlays to see how well they could be followed.

As everyone was taking their seats Mrs. Armstrong introduced Bob and Arty and her nephew Craig to the small gathering who were settled back in chairs and couches, and Mr. Hamilton opened up the evening with a prayer, and then went right into his presentation.

The Case of the Skeptic Doctor

"This is the second week in our survey of some of Creation's incredible proofs, and if you will recall from our last session we were discussing the fossil record and noting some very serious problems with the Evolutionary scheme as far as fossils are concerned. If you remember, the general theory of Evolution is supposed to show a progression of simpler life forms evolving and changing eventually into more complex animal forms...beginning with nonliving matter somehow turning into living matter or protozoan... and then from them evolving into more complex creatures and then into invertebrates or animals without back bones... and then to fish and then from fish to amphibians and from amphibians to reptiles, and then from reptiles to birds... and birds evolving into fur bearing creatures, and then into apes, and at last the apes evolving into man."

"Now as we said, if Evolution actually happened, it is logical that we should find vast numbers of transitional forms of these creatures in fossils. For example, we should find in the millions of fossils that we have, thousands of

A Creation Bible Study

these transitional forms. We should find reptiles that were half birds or at least bird-like reptiles in various stages of development, or on down the chain we should find thousands of half ape and half man-like creatures. However, as we noted, this is not the case at all, and the transitional forms from one group to the next are entirely missing in every case. For example, the transitionals from invertebrate to vertebrates are completely missing; there has never been one example found. This in itself is absolutely amazing since Evolutionists propose 100 million years of development time between the two...we should find millions or at least thousand of transitional forms of part vertebrates and part invertebrates, Yet not one such creature of any likeness this way has ever been found. Similarly there are no transitional forms of fish-like creatures turning into amphibians or amphibians into reptiles, and nothing resembling a transition between reptiles and mammals. The complete absence of any of these "link creatures" is in itself an obvious telltale blow to the Evolutionary idea. And we have deposits of millions of fossils of all sorts of creatures in various places around the world. One of them is right down here in Maryland, and yet among all the millions of fossils that are there, we have not found one example of a "link creature" bridging between any of these groups. This fact alone is a very strong argument against Evolution.

"But this week I would like to talk about some other rather obvious and uncomfortable observations that puts into serious question this imaginary idea of evolution, and the first has to do with the population of our planet.

"Our Bibles tell us that in the beginning, God made two people Adam and Eve. But those who question Creation try to argue how can we have so many people on the earth today with beginning with only two people?

"If we carefully study our Bible, we realize that it teaches that our world began about 6000 years ago when God created Adam and Eve. If our population today is say 6 billion people, the question arises, would 6000 years be enough time for there to be so many people? Well the answer as you shall see is absolutely yes!" Mr. Hamilton said looking up from his notes with a smile.

A Creation Bible Study

"But, of course, we know from our Bibles that the population started over again after the flood with Noah and his three sons and their wives. Most Creation scientists set the time of the flood about 4500 years ago, so that makes our present population sound even more impossible, doesn't it?

"One of the arguments that Evolutionists use to try to make the Bible account seem ridiculous is that they say, 'How could we have so many people in the world today if it started out with just 2 people about 6 thousand years ago?' Evolutionists believe that man has been around for at least a million years, but the Bible account describes a much, much shorter time of only 6ooo years or so.

"So let's look at this objection for a few minutes and do some simple math. Scientists estimate, even taking into account diseases, famines, disasters and wars, that the world's population doubles about every 40 years. But we can't be certain that the world's population has always doubled that often. So to be on the safe side, let's assume that the world's population doubled not every 40 years but every 150 years. In just

The Case of the Skeptic Doctor

4800 years the world's population would have doubled 32 times. If we started with just 2 people and double this 32 times, the population of the world would be about 8 and a half billion people which is more than we have on the earth today. But if the flood was around 2500 B.C. and we add approximately 2000 years to that time since Christ until today, we come up with 4500 years; so there would be 30 doublings instead of 32 giving our world's population of 6 or 7 billion which is just about what we have on the earth today if population doubled approximately every 150 years.

"But just to show the absurdity of man being around for millions of years instead of just 6 thousand years how many people would there be on the earth if they doubled every 150 years for nearly a million years? The number would be too large to even imagine. So let's say that man has been around instead of 1 million years, for just 50 thousand years instead of 6 thousand years... do you know how many people would be on the earth if the population doubled every 150 years for 50 thousand years? There would

A Creation Bible Study

have been 332 doublings instead of 32 doublings, and this gives a population that would be a 1 followed by 100 zeros and that's a really big number, a number so large we can't even imagine. Not a 1000 billion people or even a 100 trillion or a zillion people," Mr. Hamilton laughed and said, "and so where are all these people or the graves for all these people or their skeletons? It is obvious that man has not been around for millions of years, not even a hundred thousand years or even 10,000 years. But about 4500 years since the flood and with doubling even every 150 years this would give us a population about what we have on the earth today. So you see, the Bible account actually fits very accurately as an historical proof for the population of our present world."

    Bob glanced over towards Arty who returned an understanding nod at this point Mr. Hamilton made, but Arty had noticed that Craig seemed to be gazing about the room with lack of interest as Mr. Hamilton spoke.

    Mr. Hamilton continued his discussion for nearly an hour, and then the group was opened up for questions and comments; and then

The Case of the Skeptic Doctor

finally the evening's teaching came to a close.

There were refreshments on the kitchen counter, and Bob had some short discussions with a couple of dads, while Arty was talking at length with Craig, and then Bob spoke a moment with Mrs. Armstrong. "Has your nephew shown interest in the teachings on Creation?"

She returned a disheartening glance and said, "Not really... he goes to church at his mother's urging, but I'm afraid he hasn't seemed to have made a real commitment to Christ either. I don't think their church preaches that. I think he's a lot like his father, just a very good man and of high moral character, very intelligent and cares about people, but I don't think he's made any real deep commitment to God. My husband, Lee, before he passed away, tried to open up the Gospel to him a couple of times, but I don't think he understood it...please keep praying for him that he'll realize there is something deeper than just going to church."

Bob nodded with understanding.

Finally it was time to go, and as Bob and Arty were going for their car, Craig called over, "There's a diner just on the other side of the

A Creation Bible Study

Crown Point bridge...how about a hot chocolate to hold us over for our drive back to Burlington?"

"Sure," Bob smiled back, and soon they were on their way.

Bob filled Arty in on Craig's status with the Lord, and Arty answered, "Boy, he's a really nice guy! I enjoyed talking with him...he knows quite a bit about missions work, and if I hadn't heard what you just said, I would have thought for sure he was a Christian. Let's pray for each other that we can say something really meaningful to him at the diner."

Chapter 3

Diner Discussion

Cheeseburgers and french fries ended up being the fare for the hungry trio, and after Arty offered a blessing Craig was the first to begin.

"Do you guys really believe all this Creation stuff like we heard tonight?"

Bob looked up somewhat surprised and with a gentle smile returned, "Sure we do, Craig, I mean just like we heard tonight about the world's population, it is so much easier to believe the Bible than Evolution. It takes more faith to believe that it just all happened by a big chance or coincidental collision of some atoms somehow coming together and creating life...but are you having some struggles with believing

The Case of the Skeptic Doctor

it?" he tactfully inquired.

"Well, I sorta believed in Creation when I was younger, although my dad was skeptical, and when I got into the university and started sitting under these highly intelligent science and anthropology teachers who had their doctorates and who had spent their lives studying Evolution...and with so many of my pre-med classmates believing in Evolution, I guess I started doubting Creation," Craig continued, as Bob and Arty let him talk.

"I mean Professor Daniels, he was my first Anthro teacher, he presented to the class some of the proofs of the missing link, like the Piltdown Man."

Bob looked over to Arty as they were familiar with some of the so-called "missing link" hoaxes that had gotten so much publicity in many universities. Then Craig continued, "I mean the professor was so convincing he almost made it sound like only simpletons believed in Creation."

Now Bob and Arty had learned to be gentle with skeptics who came up with such attacks against Bible-believing Christians, but

Diner Discussion

Craig's remark got a little under Arty's skin so he began to explain, "Craig, we're not in any way trying to belittle your professor, but a lot of them out there want to believe their theory so much that they refuse to even look at the data that refutes those so-called 'missing link' finds, and many other obvious things."

"Oh," Craig returned.

"Yeah," Arty went on, "like the story of this 'Piltdown Man' that was supposed to have been found in the early years of this century over in England by an amateur fossil collector. And he said he had found some bones and teeth and some primitive implements, and he took them to a museum over there, and they were claimed to be 500,000 years old. Soon it was being written up in journals everywhere and talked about in museums and put into textbooks everywhere. I guess there were more than five hundred doctoral theses written about this amazing find, and everybody thought this would at last prove that Evolution was real. But about 10 years ago it was written up in Readers Digest and some other science magazines titled 'The Great Piltdown Man Hoax'!"

The Cas of th Skeptic Doctor

"Hoax...Really!" Craig retorted with big eyes.

"That's right," Arty continued, "and may I ask if that professor of yours was an older man?"

"Well, yeah, he is...that's why I trusted what he was teaching."

"Well, that's what we mean about some of the teachers on this wanting so much to believe it, especially some of the older men who have been teaching it for years...it's pretty hard to admit you've been way off and leading young people astray for years with unfounded science."

"So what was the hoax about it?" Craig listened in urgent curiosity as he devoured his hamburger.

"Well, when they looked into things more deeply, they discovered that the jaw bone found was actually that of an ape that had died about fifty years earlier. The teeth were filed down and discolored to make them look older, and they were put in the pit by this guy who was trying to believe in Evolution, too, but was disturbed by the fact that no missing links of any real scientific value had ever been found, so he was trying

Diner Discussion

to prop up the theory by fabricating the first so-called missing link."

"Really," Craig shook his head, "but what about the Nebraska Man and the Neanderthal Man? Aren't they pretty strong proofs? I mean they're pictured in a lot of reliable textbooks."

"Yeah, we know," said Bob with a perturbed smile entering into the conversation to add to his brother's comments. "But I'm sorry to inform you that the Nebraska Man is a similar fabrication by some men who so much want to believe in their theory. You know the Nebraska Man was completely constructed by artists from one tooth that was found."

"Just one tooth?" Craig sounded incredulous.

"That's right."

"How could you have any idea what a man looked like by just one tooth?" Craig said, as he drenched his french fries with ketchup.

"That's what we mean, Craig, you really can't even come close for sure, and yet they have pictures in textbooks portraying an entire race of ape-people all from this one tooth. And by the way, it was this Nebraska Man that ended up

The Case of the Skeptic Doctor

being used by so-called 'scientific experts' in the famous Scopes Monkey Trial, as it began to be called, in Tennessee back in the 1920's, when those so-called 'scientists' made a mockery of William Jennings Bryan when he said he thought the evidence was too scanty to prove Evolution. But they said, who was he to question the world's expert scientist on the subject."

"But," Arty went on, "just a few years after the trial the entire skeleton of the animal that the tooth was from was found, and do you know what the Nebraska Man was constructed from?"

"What?"

"It was from the skeleton of some pig, some rare extinct kind of pig! The so-called experts had constructed not only the Nebraska Man but an entire race of men from the tooth of a pig! Need I say when this was found out to be true there were some embarassed experts. But most people don't even know about this big error...it was just swept under the rug by the Evolutionists!"

Craig nodded as he was beginning to wonder if he had just been blindly believing what

Diner Discussion

he had been taught.

"And the Neanderthal Man and those Cro-Magnon men are fully human, and not really part ape at all, and DNA tests show there is no Ape DNA in them at all. Their thick brows and thicker bones are just characteristics of that particular race much like the different characteristics in differenet races we have today."

"Craig," Bob continued, "Mr. Hamilton was telling the truth tonight...there has not been one real 'missing link' ever found between any species, and, as he said, there should be literally millions if not at least thousands of intermediate examples showing the transition from one to another form, but they're just not there!"

"Huh, I didn't realize that they have so little real proof for what they so adamently teach as absolute fact," Craig admitted.

"No, they really don't," Bob affimed.

Craig was thinking, and then he said, "I've always wanted to believe the Bible, and don't get me wrong, I'm a Christian, I mean I go to church every week and try to be kind to people and I've even tried to read the Bible, but I have to admit I have a little trouble understanding it

The Case of th Skeptic Doctor

in places...and I don't want to sound like I'm being argumentative, and I don't want to offend you guys or doubt your sincerity, but I struggle to believe some of those impossible things in the Bible, especially like the flood and all those animals. How in the world could all the world's animals fit on a little boat?"

Bob smiled and then continued, "Well, in the first place, that was no little boat. The actual size Creation scientists affirm of the Ark was similar to that of some of our ocean-going barges today, somewhere between 450 and 600 feet long, and it was three stories high...they estimate that two of all the world's species could comfortably fit on less that half the Ark's capacity, giving more than ample room for food for all those animals, plus for Noah and his sons and their wives. Sometime I'll have to give you a good book on the flood and the Ark that I've got... it's pretty fascinating how logical it all is."

"Yeah, I'd like to read it," Craig said sounding open to taking another look at what he had so long questioned as true, but then he said, "But what about stories like the walls of Jericho falling flat merely from the shouts of some

Diner Discussion

people? I've always had trouble believing that."

"Well, you know the Bible is full of miracles that seem impossible, but remember it is God we are talking about. And, Craig, did you know our father Jesse Baxter was an avid Evolutionist before he found the Lord as his Savior?"

"Oh, really, I didn't know that."

Bob elaborated,"Yep, but he came to believe some of the seemingly impossible miracles in the Bible had to be true, because of the miracle that happened to him the night he came to Christ."

"Really, what do you mean? Tell me about it, if it's not getting too late for you fellas. I'm curious."

"My dad when going to college had a close friend who had his master's degree in archeology," Bob began to tell the story, "and this friend of his majored in Evolution. Well, one Saturday, my dad was helping his friend move to another city where he was going to run a museum in that large metropolitan area. While they were driving along together in the moving truck discussing Evolution, my dad knowing of his

The Case of the Skeptic Doctor

friend Steve's knowledge of that subject had one perplexing difficulty with Evolution... the 'missing links', and so he just said to his friend Steve casually, 'Why don't they just lay out the missing link examples on a table somewhere so that we can see all the transition forms?' You see my dad, like your dad and so many others, just assumed they were around and the theory was true and well proven, just like you have thought. But Steve's reply totally surprised my father. Steve said, 'Well that's one thing they are having a little trouble being able to do.' My dad didn't know how to respond so he just replied, 'Oh', but he wondered why Steve didn't give a lengthy discussion about how abundant and well-founded those missing links were, but later my dad realized that Steve didn't discuss that in detail because they really don't have them...they didn't have them then, and they don't have them now."

"Wow...so what changed your dad's mind about it?" Craig said sounding open.

"Some months later my dad was invited to go hear some Christian businessmen speak at a Gospel banquet. And that night he was at a point in his life where he felt there must be more

Diner Discussion

to life than trying to simply build a big business and become wealthy. He actually had a longing to know if there was a God. That night a couple of Christian businessmen explained that the Bible teaches that you can know God in a personal way, that you can have your sins forgiven and that Christ will come directly into your very life and physical body by His Spirit....my dad was listening intently, and different Bible verses were shared that night, but one of them that caught his attention was Revelation 3:20. Here let me show it to you," Bob said reaching in his back pocket for his New Testament, and thumbing through to the page.

"Here it is, 'Behold I stand at the door and knock. If any one hears my voice and opens the door.'.. like the door of your heart and life," Bob said looking over to Craig, "Jesus said, 'I will come into him. and sup with him and he with me.' That's describing an intimate spiritual closeness," Bob explained going on. "My dad didn't understand it all that night, but he knew he needed Christ and His forgiveness, and so in a brief prayer of faith he opened the door inviting Jesus into his life, by faith. My dad

The Case of the Skeptic Doctor

was completely surprised with the change that came over him as God's Spirit came upon him...he had this overwhelming sense that God was at last with him, just like the Bible said, that Christ would come into his physical body and life...so after this happened, and not long after that, my father thought, 'Why wouldn't all the teachings and stories in the Bible be true if this one amazing experience of the indwelling Spirit was true?' You see, the other miracles of the Bible didn't seem all that impossible to my dad now that he had experienced this first incredible miracle of Christ coming into his life that the Bible describes."

"Interesting," Craig said pondering.

"Craig," Bob said with sincerity, "most people don't believe in the miracles of the Bible until they see the miracle of having Christ come into their lives that the Bible teaches. When that miracle happens then they begin to understand that the other seemingly impossible things in the Bible must also be true...and, Craig, being a Christian isn't just deciding you are going to try to live a good life or do good to others...there's nothing wrong with that, but it doesn't make you

Diner Discussion

one of Christ's. It isn't trying to be a Christian, it is rather surrendering to the Lordship of Christ, and then He comes into our lives and works His work in us. The night my dad found God there wasn't anything even said about Evolution. Those men just talked about knowing Christ in a personal way, and that's what my dad wanted. And then after he came to know the Lord and began to re-think his opinions about Evolution, he realized that Creation explains so clearly and more logically so many things that the Evolutuionary model can't begin to explain."

"So do you guys believe in Creation, since your dad does?" Craig asked innocently.

Bob explained, "We both found Christ as young boys and knew the joys of being 'born again' and having the presence of God's Spirit in our hearts. And as teenagers as a part of our home schooling, we studied the contrast between Creation and Evolution, and can tell you that Creation is much easier and more logical to believe, and there are many many more proofs similar to what you heard tonight from Mr. Hamilton that will help you to see the truth of Creation... I hope you can come back in a couple of weeks."

"I'm looking forward to it," Craig replied.

"We better run now," Bob said as he reached for the bill.

"Oh, you don't need to pick up the tab, Bob, here let me get it," Craig said reaching out.

"We'll get it, Craig," Arty smiled.

"Okay, but I'll pick up the tip," he said as he reached into his pocket.

"Thanks, Craig," said Bob, "see you in a couple weeks at your aunt's?"

"Sure, sure, why not? I've got a couple more weeks of classes, and then I'm all done for the summer, but, Bob, Arty, I want you to know I'm going to be thinking about these things you've shared tonight, and where is that in the Bible about being 'born again', I think that's what you called it, where the Holy Spirit comes into our lives?"

"Oh...it's in John, Chapter 3," came Bob's quick reply.

"Now if I can just find my Bible," Craig grinned. "I haven't looked at it for years," he admitted as they went out of the cafe.

Chapter 4

A Call to Action!

The two weeks zoomed by, and Bob and Arty, having told their family about their last visit to the Creation science session at Mrs. Armstrong's and a little more about Craig's openness to the Gospel, were eager to return. And they had no sooner climbed out of their Scout at Mrs. Armstrong's when Craig waved from the empty porch and started coming their way carrying his Bible and wearing a warm smile; evidently he had been waiting for them. They couldn't help but wonder if something new had happened in his life.

"Found my Bible," he said with a big grin, "and I've been enjoying the Gospel of John and some other places in it, but I'll have to tell you more later. I think they're ready to get started." Bob and Arty were running late, everybody was inside, and the session was just about to begin. Mrs. Armstrong met Bob and Arty and gave them a quick report of some urgent needs with Dr. Armstrong down in western Brazil in the Amazon Jungle medical clinic.

She quickly explained, "Craig just handed me this letter from his dad that his father had sent weeks ago but finally came though the mail today. It seems to be a confirmation to my thoughts about trying to send you young men down there, I mean if you are open to the idea...and Craig said he wanted you to read the letter."

"Good," said Bob as she handed it to him. "We've been praying about everything for two weeks and feel it is the Lord's will."

Mr. Hamilton was soon into his presentation, and to their surprise Bob and Arty noticed keen interest this time from Criag; but their minds were in a swirl thinking about the call to action they had just received from Mrs. Armstrong. Bob could hardly pay attention as he was skimming through the letter Mrs.

A Call to Action!

Armstrong had just given him from her brother-in-law, Dr. Wes Armstrong.

Bob noticed that the letter to Craig mentioned how his dad wondered if his brother might be able to help them out in Brazil. "Poor man," Bob thought, "he thinks his brother is still alive."

As he quickly read through the letter not trying to seem rude with Mr. Hamilton's presentation, Bob was trying to recall how well stocked up they were with emergency supplies for flood victims. That was the gist of the letter. The doctor's clinic and surrounding areas in the Amazon forest had been innundated with rain and flooding, and their landing strip was now completely under water making them unable to get in or out. There were nearby tribes that were completely cut off by the flood, and the doctor feared they were in a desperate situation. It would be impossible to reach them, and their only hope was to try to drop supplies from the air, but he could get no help from the government which had enough problems of their own dealing with the extensive flooding. The government wasn't concerned about those small tribes in remote corners of the jungle. Wes closed

The Case of the Skeptic Doctor

the letter by telling Craig that he remembered that somehow he knew that Mr. Baxter's boys had started up a mission aid service and were flying an old DC3 that their dad used to use for his freight business, and he didn't know if that would be of any possibility, but was hoping Craig might check into that with his Aunt and Uncle Armstrong. Bob handed the letter to Arty as Bob tried to catch up with the topic of discussion. It was on the "hoax missing links", and so Bob knew most of what he was sharing and was glad to have Mr. Hamilton reinforcing some of the things they had told Craig two weeks before at the diner.

A good 30 minutes passed in discussing some of those fake "missing links", and then Mr. Hamilton shifted his discussion to some of the incredible phenomena in the animal kingdom that completely defies the Evolutionary idea.

"For example," Hamilton said, "let's take a look at the migratory instincts of birds and animals. Instincts are nearly impossible to explain by the Evolutionary model. For example, the white throated warbler. It summers in Germany but winters in Africa. As the summer comes to a

A Call to Action!

close in Germany, the newborn baby birds are getting older and are completely left behind by the parent birds who take off for Africa. Several weeks later the new generation takes off and flies instinctively across thousands of miles of unfamiliar land and sea and rejoins their parents in Africa! How do they manage to navigate so precisely to re-join their parents over such distances without having ever flown that course before with their parents? Other birds like the barn swallow migrate thousands of miles from Canada to Argentina. The Arctic turn flies 14,000 miles back and forth each year from the North Pole to the South Pole and back again. Evolutionists have a hard time trying to come up with some explanation of how these abilities somehow evolved gradually over millions of years. This seems highly improbable because migratory instincts are useless unless they are perfectly performed each time from the very first time, or the species would perish! The entire species would disappear if they had to learn instincts in incremental steps, like going half way across the ocean as Evolution suggests."

Craig's attention was fixed on the dis-

The Case of the Skeptic Doctor

cussion as Mr. Hamilton talked of the migratory instincts of insects like the Monarch butterfly that lays eggs that become caterpillars that eventually spin cocoons, inside of which it goes through metamorphosis, emerges as a beautiful butterfly, which in itself speaks of an amazing intelligent design, and then somehow knows to fly well over 10,000 miles to its ancestral wintering grounds in Mexico. The perfection of migratory instincts and all its intricacies, and its vital role in the preservation of thousands of animals, and insects, and birds cannot be explained by a gradual learning or an evolving process; they had to have the complete guidance system already implanted in their minds when they were born or they would have died off. Of course, the Evolutionist always tries to make the impossible seem possible by saying if we had millions or billions of years then it might have happened, but as we explained last week there is absolutely no evidence of an old earth, and, in fact, the evidence we have points strongly to a young earth of 6 thousand years young or so. The only logical explanation is that these animals were wisely and carefully designed or created with these impressive migratory abilities placed in them by God so that they could live enjoyable and successful lives generation after generation."

In a little while Mr. Hamilton brought his insightful presentation to a close and quoted from Romans 1:20, "'For the invisible things of Him from the Creation of the world are clearly seen, being understood by the things that are made, even His eternal power and Godhead; so that they are without excuse.' You see, friends, God does these 'invisible things that are clearly seen' so that we might seek after that all-wise, invisible Creator God, and He has given so many amazing examples of His hidden presence just to see if there is any man out there who is seeking to find Him; and those that are seeking He helps to find. Evolution is just a cleverly devised excuse that so many conveniently use so that they don't think they are accountable to a Creator or have any need to seek after Him or even have Him in their minds."

Mr. Hamilton paused and then said, "Let's pray," and Mr. Hamilton gave an invitation for anyone who was seeking to open his heart and invite Jesus to come into their lives, would pray along with him. There were a couple folks from down the street who were visiting, and Mr. Hamilton had them in mind when giving the invitation.

Following the discussion the group enjoyed some refreshments, and Bob and Arty were expressing their desire to head out as soon as possible for the Amazon jungle to bring aid to the flood-ravaged region. They had no sooner told their intentions to Mrs. Armstrong when Craig who was standing beside her spoke up, "Bob, Arty, I don't know if I would be of any help...I might just be in the way, but I do know quite a bit about my dad's situation down there... every couple months except for this last winter, for nearly 7 years, I've gotten a letter from Dad telling me all sorts of different things about his work and the people down there. He has even sent me a detailed map of his location and the surrounding jungles and lots of other descriptions of his work that might help us locate them."

"That sounds like an answer to prayer," said Arty. "We've tried to locate tribal villages in that region before, and it can be like trying to find a needle in a haystack. It seems to me your

A Call to Action!

input would be very helpful," he added smiling to Craig.

Then Craig continued in a rather shy but encouraged manner, "But there's something even more that has happened in my life with God, that I've been wanting to tell you about since our last visit at the diner."

"Oh...good," said Bob. "We'd like to hear it."

"And I would, too," Mrs. Armstrong said turning to Craig with a smile.

By now most of the guests had said goodbye for the evening, and Mrs. Armstrong suggested the fellas have a seat around her kitchen table to talk.

Craig was excited to tell his story. "When I got home last time we talked, I tried to remember where I might have put my Bible, and then I recalled a few boxes of books that were on the floor in back of my coat closet...and the very first one I opened, there it was lying on the very top. And I sat down and was looking for John, Chapter 3 and found it. I was surprised to realize the story was about a religious man named Nicodemus, and I have one of those Bibles that

The Case of the Skeptic Doctor

has a commentary at the bottom, and the comment was about how Nicodemus was afraid to go to Jesus by day for fear of what the other religious men he knew would think of him. And that made me think of myself and how I know among so many of my intellectual friends, and even church-going friends, being a follower of Jesus is sometimes made fun of. So right away I could relate to this man Nicodemus. But then I noticed how he was called by Jesus a 'master of Israel', and the commentary said he was a leading religious teacher of the Scriptures; but Jesus said to him that he should have known that a man must be 'born again' to enter the kingdom of God. And this made me think about what you guys told me two weeks ago, about how being a Christian wasn't trying to be good or even going to church. And I realized that maybe I was a lot like Nicodemus. I mean I've been kinda a religious man and even faithfully gone to church, but I didn't know this most important thing about being 'born again' or being 'born of the Spirit' as Jesus called it in that context...like you guys told me about what had happened to you as boys and your dad. So I just laid there in my bed

A Call to Action!

reading the story over and over, and that verse that many people know, the one that says, 'For God so loved the world that He gave His only begotten Son that whosoever believeth in Him should not perish but have everlasting life' was right there! And I was trying to think if I had ever believed in Jesus...and I guess I knew somewhat about Him, but I didn't think I really had believed in Him. I laid there for a long time, and I kept feeling like I wanted to know God like you guys do, and then I remembered that verse you shared about Jesus standing at the door of our lives and how if we open the door and invited Him in He would answer. So I folded my hands, and I just said as sincerely as I could, 'Jesus, help me to believe... I'm opening the door of my life to You... I'm not holding back any of it...if You will make me Your own, then I will follow You and serve You the rest of my life.' But then I started thinking who was I to be a friend of Jesus, and I started feeling really badly about myself...I mean my sins and my selfish life, and so I quietly asked Him to forgive me of all my sins, and then after that I had this strange peace come over me. And that's the last thing I

The Case of the Skeptic Doctor

remember, but when I woke up the next morning I still had this peace, and I started to think about God and it gave me joy."

Mrs. Armstong was quietly listening, and tears welled up in her eyes; she had prayed for him for many years.

Bob spoke softly, "That's wonderful, Craig."

And Arty said with a kind smile, "That's good, Craig...real good."

"Well, that's not all...when I left my place to walk to one of my classes, I ran into a guy that I used to detest about as much as anybody, and normally I would do my best to ignore him. I mean he's kinda obnoxious and thinks he's the smartest guy in the world, if you know what I mean. Well, he was right beside me heading to class, but instead of disliking him I had this strange kindness for him and my heart went out for him. And then moments later he hurried off... he had forgotten something, but as I continued on walking I thought, 'This is strange of me. I have a new love...I'm different.' I looked up at the trees and the birds and the beautiful blue sky, and it was all so lovely to me, and I whispered

A Call to Action!

to God, 'You have made all these things, and thank you for helping me and making me new inside.' And that's the way I've been now for almost two weeks."

"That's wonderful," Mrs Armstrong said, reaching out to give him a little hug. "I'm so happy for you."

"Thanks, Auntie, I'm so happy, too, and that presentation tonight was good...I can't wait to learn more of the amazing things of God."

Bob and Arty rejoiced to see the wonderful change in their new friend's life, and were eager to spend some time with him on their upcoming mission. "Do you think you could leave next Monday for the Amazon region?" Bob asked.

"Sounds good to me! I'm looking forward to it," Craig replied. "But first I want to drive down to Boston and see my mom and see if she has anything to send down to dad. Mom could never handle the work down in Brazil, and so dad goes down for the winters and she helps out at the clinic in Boston. She's been real worried about him this winter since she hasn't heard from him for weeks now, but figures that he

The Case of the Skeptic Doctor

hasn't been able to get his mail out to her with the flooding down there. And I also want to try to say a few words to her about my new relathionship with the Lord."

"We'll be praying for you, Craig, and see you next week, Lord willing," Bob said as he drew up a little map for Craig to use to drive out to the Air-Truck terminal in Essex where they were going to set to work getting ready for a departure as soon as all could be loaded up in Old Gabe, their transport DC3.

"I often go down to see my mom on weekends, but I'll be back about noon on Monday and see you then!" Craig said saying goodbye to his new friends.

The evening ended, and the brothers rejoiced together on their way home that night, thanking God that they had been given the boldness to share with Craig the little bit they did, although they both felt they had done a pretty poor job of it; nevertheless, they were eager to tell their family of Craig's decision for Christ when they got home.

Chapter 5

Off to the Amazon

"Those are real signs that Craig has come to the faith," said Jesse Baxter as the family gathered in the kitchen for breakfast. "When you see the 'fruit of the Spirit' in a person's life, then you can be pretty sure it was a genuine conversion to Christ. Sometimes a young person will make an emotional commitment even praying and trying to be as sincere as they can, but without the working of the Holy Spirit in the heart there is no real conversion," he added as breakfast was being served up and then said, "Sometimes a person will begin to try to be faithful with things like reading the Bible and going to church, and they may even learn a few verses and enjoy singing hymns as they try to feel within themselves they are at peace with God, but in

The Case of the Skeptic Doctor

time many lose their interest, or they just go about a religious life in an intellectual way, filling their minds with Bible facts, and learning the right theology trying to convince themselves and others that they are children of God. But it is so much better when you see the fruits that the Holy Spirit produces like faith in, and a love for, Jesus, and having a desire to see others come to Christ... and to be drawn to the Word of God...when you see these things then you can be pretty sure it's genuine."

"You know, Dad," Arty said, "you don't have to be an expert evangelist when the Lord is working in a man's heart...God just helps him seek, doesn't He?"

"Yeah, that's good, Arty...we need to just be willing to share Christ as the Lord leads, and then let the results be in God's hands," Jesse added.

"I was reading this morning in Timothy," Josh joined in as he reached out to take a piece of jelly toast from the serving plate, "and saw where Paul said he was 'persuaded' that the faith that was in Timothy's Mother and Grandmother was in Timothy also, and I was wondering if

Off To The Amazon

Timothy was one of those who didn't know the exact date when he got saved, but Paul could see the genuine fruits of the faith in his life."

"Yeah, that's probably true," Jesse agreed.

Then Bessy commented, " Grandma once told me she didn't know the exact day she was saved...she just knows that she believes with all her heart in Jesus."

"We can all tell Grandma loves the Lord and is full of faith, can't we?" Mother smiled.

They all agreed, and Father said, "So we'll be praying for your trip down to Brazil. I'm sure you will be an encouragement to Craig, and hopefully you will be able to reach out to his father. Sounds like he's one of those kind who has really tried to be a Christian, by doing good deeds, and trying to live sacrificially, and having compassion for the plight of needy people, but sometimes those things can make you think you have earned a way to be okay with God. But when the Spirit of God brings conviction for sin, and feelings of lostness, and the need for forgiveness, then all those good works of self-goodness seem useless and empty."

The Case of the Skeptic Doctor

The spiritual talk around the dinner table was most always uplifting for the Baxter family, and soon they finished up and the guys headed over to the Air/Truck terminal to stock up Old Gabe. Arty kept watching every so often for Craig's Chevy to pull in. For some reason, he was late, but then finally a half hour before take off Craig came racing in. Parking, he grabbed his luggage and was heading for the building.

Greetings shared with Craig were warm but somewhat brief, as Craig apologized for running late. Father informed Bob and Arty that Rusty their father's chief mechanic, and their younger brother Josh, had given the DC3 a thorough going through just last week, and all systems were good to go. Rusty said he had a feeling that the Lord was going to call them to service soon, Jesse said. The Baxter's were all at the Air/Truck hanger, and the girls went through the final checklist in the storage room as the fellas finished loading supplies onboard the plane, securing them in their proper places. They carefully packed all the medical supplies for sicknesses and diseases that are all too common in the tropics. Bags of rice and other food com-

Off to the Amazon

modities were put onboard. Bedding and blankets, tents and cooking equipment were put into separate bundles with packets of food with hopes they could be parachute-dropped to the stranded tribesmen and their families. Finally they were about ready to board the plane when old Grandpa and Grandma Baxter came walking in the Air-Truck hanger where they were gathered.

"We saw a couple of items we thought you might need," Gramps said smiling while he and Grandma were introduced to Craig. Gramps handed Arty his old double-barrel shotgun and a box of shells. "Didn't know if this might be useful in the jungle...you never know what kind of critters you might run into down there, and for some reason this old relic keeps sliding down in my closet, and I thought I'd get rid of it, so if you accidentally drop it in the river, it won't matter," he said grinning handing it to Arty.

"Thanks, Gramps, I know those jungle guides always take guns with 'em just in case."

"And since it will be your birthday while you're gone, Arty," Gramps added, "I saw this little hikers pocket compass, too, the other day, and I know how confusing it can be in trying to

The Case of the Skeptic Doctor

keep your bearing in dense jungle undergrowth so thought it might come in handy... and it even has a 'glow in the dark' direction needle, and the North, South, East, West points glow, too."

"Neat...thanks, Gramps," Arty smiled, studying the device.

Then grinning Grandma handed them each a bottle of mosquito repellent. "I saw this in the General Store last night, and when we heard about your new mission and I saw this repellent that we liked last year, I thought of you... it doesn't have any dangerous chemicals in it, and I also thought, if it works good enough in Vermont I know it will work good enough anywhere in the world!" she added with a little giggle. The brothers thanked their thoughtful grandparents as just then the girls were coming over with hands clutching big picnic baskets full of something.

Mom smiled as the boys gazed at the baskets, "The girls stayed up late last night making emergency survival cookies, sandwiches and some other goodies that they figured the missionary team might need." The guys smiled with appreciation.

Off to the Amazon

Then Josh who had been busy loading up the plane said, "I don't imagine those cookies will survive very long." Everybody laughed.

Finally with everything ready they gathered around in a circle, and Jesse offered a prayer for their safe and successful mission; and he prayed especially that someone's life may be changed through their efforts.

Climbing aboard, Bob and Arty took the pilot seats in front while Craig settled into the navigator's seat behind them. Within minutes the plane was towed out of the hanger by Josh, and then the engines were cranked over, first the left and then the right, as they began to increase in RPM's warming up. Arty was checking their flight plan while Bob toggled through the different systems verifying that all was in good running order, while Craig watched on at the interesting pre-flight check out.

The kind voice of Grant Smith their Air/Truck air traffic controller soon came over the cockpit radio from the control tower. "Come in Flight J 3:16...this is the controller's deck."

Reaching for his mic Arty clicked it on raising it to his mouth, "Roger, come in, Grant,

The Case of the Skeptic Doctor

good to hear your voice... over."

"Roger, I've been praying for you, and all's clear to go with everything down here, as long as you feel everything is cleared from Above," Grant said with reassurance.

"Thanks, Grant, we've checked it out with the Great Navigator as best we can, and we have a peace about it and feel strengthened to go...it seems to be His plan... over."

"Good, all clear for taxying and take-off whenever you're ready...and God's speed...we'll be praying, and see you as soon as you're able to return... over and out..."

"God's blessings to you, too, from the crew of Flight J3:16...over and out," Arty replied clicking off his mic.

Within minutes Old Gabe was climbing into the cool late morning sky heading south down along the spine of the Green Mountains. Craig was fascinated and quiet as Bob and Arty skillfully brought the plane to cruising altitude on the flight plan to Atlanta where they would stop and refuel. From there they would hop over the Gulf of Mexico heading south for the Amazon River western region.

Off to the Amazon

After a while Craig took his eyes off the landscape unfolding below and was gazing at the cockpit in front with all its interesting dials and gauges and instruments. Craig was some-

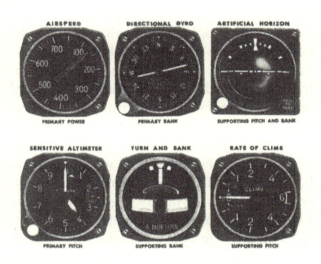

Craig took his eyes off the landscape unfolding below and was gazing at the cockpit in front with all its interesting dials and gauges and instruments.

what familiar with flying, having flown his father's Beechcraft many times, but that flying machine was small and unsophisticated compared to this larger DC3. "This plane is pretty well equipped," Craig said feeling a little challenged with the various flight instrumentation they didn't have on his Dad's plane.

"Well," Bob began, "we have updated the cockpit features with a good bit of more advanced avionics. We even replaced the old control yokes with these more comfortable modern units," Bob said with hands firmly on the steering yoke. Craig was fascinated with the detailed description Bob gave of some of the gauges in front of them. Finally, after a while, the plane had entered an uncongested part of their flight, and so Arty took the liberty to go back and give Craig a more thorough tour of their flying ship. He showed Craig how different things worked in the galley or kitchen and then the sleeping quarters and then the nice lounging area complete with their extensive Christian library.

Arty began, "I had my quiet time onboard Old Gabe this morning when I drove over early this morning to fuel her up and to go over our

Off to the Amazon

pre-flight checklist. I looked up and noticed one of our Creation books on the shelf and found an interesting quote by Charles Darwin, himself, on the surprising absence of any well defined 'missing links' in the geological fossil record of his day...it reminded me of our conversation at the diner a few weeks ago."

"Oh, yeah? I'd like to see that. I used to be a fan of Darwin," Craig said rolling his eyes.

"Sure, here, let me read it to you," Arty said as he lifted the book off the end table that was opened turned down to keep the place. Here it is a quote from Darwin, 'As by this theory (of Evolution) innumerable transition forms must have existed. Why do we not find them imbedded in the crust of the earth? Why is all nature not in confusion instead of being as we see them, well defined species? Geological research does not yield the infinitely many fine gradations between past and present species required by the theory (of Evolution), and this is one of the many objections which may be argued against it. The explanation lies, however, in the extreme imperfection of the geological record.' And by that he means the imperfect fossil record that he had in his day," Arty said and then continued, "but that was way back in the 1860's, and so Darwin assumed that as they found more and more geological fossil records, then they would eventually find those 'missing links'. But it's been over a hundred years since Darwin's time, and thousands of new geological items have been discovered, and we now have actually fewer examples of those 'missing links' than they had in his day, because, like Bob and I told you a couple weeks ago, many of those so-called 'proof examples' have ended up being nothing more than hoaxes. And so those proofs have been discarded as unreliable. Darwin thought the 'missing links' would be found, but, in fact, there has not really been one good example found anywhere in the millions of fossils that have now been discovered in the last hundred years. There should be thousands of examples of these 'missing links,' yet there isn't one single one that is even close to being reliable. Creation scientists now say that the fossil record found in the last century has been so rich in findings that it can no longer be an argument that new discoveries will reveal the 'missing link'...they should have found hundreds by now, but not one has been discovered. You see, Craig, instead what the abundance of fossil records shows is the sudden appearance of highly different and complex forms of life with no intermediate forms at all. You see the fossil record is overwhelmingly proving with each new find that God created all of these things uniquely just as the Bible says He did!" Arty expounded.

"Oh, I know, Arty... you don't have to try to convince me any more...most people are like I once was not realizing how much faith it takes to believe in Evolution. If they would just take the time to look into it they would discover how far fetched the theory really is," Craig confided.

"Oh, I know," Arty replied, "but its like what old Napoleon once said, 'People will believe anything as long as it's not in the Bible.'"

"That's so true," Craig nodded, "but I know I've got a lot to learn, and I hope you and Bob and I can have some good Bible discussions on our trip."

The next few hours went by quickly, and Arty took the controls for a while, and Bob got up and fixed them all lunch with chips and a

The Case of the Skeptic Doctor

chicken salad sandwich that Bessy had made and put on-board in the refrigerator. Resuming their places in the cock-pit, Bob and Craig rejoined Arty, and the trio enjoyed the scenery and their lunch; and finally by late afternoon they reached the approaching final descent for the Atlanta International Airport and landed smoothly and taxied to the refueling area.

Chapter 6

Over the Big Pond

As their flight carried them south of Florida, Arty took a few minutes to look over the maps with Craig who was sitting behind the cockpit in the navigator's seat. To Craig's right was a small tabletop on which the maps were laid out. Arty pointed out their flight path over the Gulf of Mexico.

"Boy, that's a big pond, isn't it?" Craig said smiling..."this rig got enough fuel to carry us over it?"

"I hope so," Arty laughed, "or we're going to make a big splash in that big pond."

Craig looked up with a dry smile.

Arty pointed out their flight plan, "We're going to have to stay away from the Cuban air space...and to arrive in western Brazil, we will

The Case of the Skeptic Doctor

go first from here to Costa Rica and re-fuel...this first flight is the longest. Then from San Jose, Costa Rica, it's about a 5 hour flight to Bogota, Colombia, where we will spend the night, and then re-fuel again and fly south in the morning to your father's mission post on the western Amazon."

"I see," Craig said following Arty's pointer over the map.

"Just curious. Why Bogota?" Craig asked.

"We're familiar a little with the airport," Arty replied, "and they, like Costa Rica, welcome Americans and their fuel prices are good...and besides, it is just 600 miles northwest of your father's medical mission. Here, take a look at the map," Arty pointed to the map.

"Oh, yeah, I see," said Craig.

"Didn't you say your father's mission was on the Rio Negro River tributary?" Arty inquired.

"That's right," Craig nodded.

"Well, you see we just descend the slopes of the northern Andes from Bogota, and head down into the Amazon Basin, and if we can't find a strip to land on in that flooded jungle, at least we can either turn around and fly back to Bogota, or go down to Manaus, Brazil, and land and then try again."

"Oh, I see your plan."

"And come to think of it," Arty continued, "we had a mission down your father's way in Colombia with an MD named Jim Pearson a while back."

"Oh, really?"

"Yeah, we'll have to tell you about that mission sometime...we ended up getting trapped in an abandoned mine."

"Hmm...sounds interesting! I guess you must have made it out somehow?" Craig said with a grin.

"Yeah, if we get bored, we'll give you the details, but now while we have some flight time on our hands how about you telling us a little about your father and his work down there in the Amazon jungle?" Bob suggested turning his head glancing back.

"Okay...let me see," Craig was thinking. "My father built up a good medical practice down near Boston when I was a boy, but he was al-

The Case of the Skeptic Doctor

ways the adventurous type, and he would leave his practice to some of the other doctors and take trips all over the world. And he would get his brother who had his practice over in upper state New York, you know Uncle Lee who just passed away last winter, to go with him. My dad and his brother Lee came from a generation of really decent people who had a passion for giving themselves for the good of mankind. I guess they both just really wanted their lives to count for something meaningful...just like I guess most people want out of life.

"And they both were the adventurous kind, and I remember as a little guy traveling with my dad and his brother and mom and Aunt Lydia to national parks all around in America. We even went up to Alaska one time and got caught in a snowstorm in late summer. We would hike and camp out and fish, and then when I was about 12 years old, Uncle Lee and Aunt Lydia started doing some 'soul searching,' as my dad used to call it. They went to some crusades, and now I know what happened to my Uncle Lee and Aunt Lydia...they both found Christ like I did a few weeks ago, but my dad could never understand it, and he thought his brother had just gotten mixed up with some 'holy rollers' as my dad used to say mocking behind their back. And then when Uncle Lee started studying some Creation science from a teacher out of California, my dad and his brother had a falling out over it. My dad always made the better grades in school and med school, and so he always thought he was smarter than his brother, and so when Uncle Lee started talking about Creation, my dad, being an avid Evolutionist, wouldn't agree with it, and they used to get into some pretty lengthy discussions and arguments about it.

"Then my mom got real sick and ended up in the hospital, and we didn't think she was going to make it, so Uncle Lee and Aunt Lydia would bring their Bibles and try to read verses to her, and she was kinda interested in their beliefs. But this really irked my Dad, and he got upset with his brother, and they had a falling out over it. When my mom got better, I think just to try to show he was just as good a Christian as his Bible-believing brother, my dad started getting involved in this humanitarian medical work he does down here in Brazil, and I think he

The Case of the Skeptic Doctor

thought he was going to prove Evolution, too, by going down there to the Amazon and studying those primitive tribesmen and visiting some archeological sites. Don't mis-understand, my dad is a real caring person and has a heart for humanity, and so he's trying to do his best with helping those folks down there with their health needs, but he has not seen any point, nor could he, as far as I know, to help them with their eternal needs. He's like so many others who just don't want to think about what the Bible says about God, and their souls, or eternity that much. And like most others he thinks that if his good outweighs his bad, then he'll be all right in the end...like I used to think."

"Yeah, Craig, it sounds like we're going to need to be real patient with your dad and not make the mistake of coming at him too strong with the Bible and Creation, and just be praying that God would work in his heart and that he might come to us with questions, because unless the Lord is beginning a good work in his heart all our efforts to convince him may just turn him against us," Arty speculated.

"And you know, Craig," Bob joined in,

"Evolution is just nothing more than a religious belief that they think is based on science, but it really isn't. It is built on faith in a kind of pseudo-science that can't be proved, and, in fact, as you know, honest science disproves it over and over again. Evolution believes everything began by chance or some big accidental explosion that resulted in complex intelligent designed life all coming about simply by a "big Kaboom!" But all the logical scientific proofs we can show them is really of no avail unless they are open to the truth. It's more a matter of the will with them than anything else, but because believing in Creation makes one accountable to a Creator, most people don't want to think about it seriously."

"Yeah, I know what you mean, and my dad knows I'm a top student so he respects me and thinks I'm on his side; so I'm not quite sure how to tell him about my new life...I don't want to upset him," Craig confided.

"How'd your mother react when you saw her? Did you get a chance to talk to her about your new faith?" Arty joined in.

"She just commented on how happy and peaceful I seemed. I used to be pretty moody and kinda fidgety. I told her I had been reading the Bible and praying more...sorry, guys, I guess I was afraid of upsetting her, so I didn't say much," Craig confided.

"It may not have been the best time, Craig. You can't push it when sharing Christ," Bob comforted.

"Oh, good, I was afraid I let the Lord down, but she did comment about a new young single lady nurse assistant at their clinic who's a 'born again Christian' Mom said, and that got my attention," Craig smiled, "and Mom said she really likes her... said she was so kind and gentle with everyone." Craig went on, "And..and..get this...this young girl named Jenn, Mom said, was even interested in missions work! She said Jenn thought God must not have plans for her to marry since she was now getting older, and so she was planning on getting some medical assistant experience so she could go to the mission field somewhere and be a doctor's assistant."

"Hmm, that's sure interesting," Bob reacted.

"Yeah, that was part of the reason I was late getting up here to Vermont yesterday," Craig confessed with a blush. "Naturally I just had to stop by my mom's clinic to say hello to the doctors.... and the staff!" he added grinning.

"Well, of course," Bob returned the grin.

"But, seriously," Craig continued, "My mom gave me an envelope of some cash that they all there at the clinic had put together and wanted to send down to contribute to my dad's work, so I can help out with our expenses."

"Thanks, Craig, but the Lord has been blessing, so just hang on to it and use it as the Lord leads, but we need to be praying for your mom and dad, and be real patient with your dad, and not beat him over the head with the Bible by sounding too preachy or 'know it all' when we get down there," Arty suggested.

"Well, there's another problem going on down there now, and that is that an old friend of my dad's has been going around to the tribes and trying to teach a 'works salvation religion' of some kind that this guy believes in, and he's been trying to teach his own twisted version of the Bible... and from what I can tell from my dad's letters, his friend has been taking advantage of the natives for their money."

The Case of the Skeptic Doctor

"Money?" Arty frowned, not understanding. "Those natives don't have any money, do they?"

"Well, they don't think of it as money, but they know of a cave or pit over in the mountains somewhere where there are diamonds."

"Diamonds!?" Arty quizzed.

"Yeah, there are a few diamond mines around in Brazil, and, in fact, about 25 years ago they found a world famous diamond called the Vargas diamond down there, and it weighed some 720 carats or about a third of a pound," Craig said.

"Wow...that's huge!" Bob declared.

"Yeah, and so in the area of my dad's compound is an old abandoned mine pit that the natives nearby my dad's compound know about, where they still find a few small stones once in a while. And this friend of my dad's, his name is Bill Paris, is always trading some cheap things like trinkets and other worthless things for those diamonds the natives find," Craig explained. "And Paris tells them he is just going to use the money they make from those diamonds to build a great temple to God somewhere down there, and so as gullible as those natives are, he's got them duped into thinking they are doing a good thing for God, and that somehow that temple is going to help them be close to God," Craig detailed.

"Oh, brother," blurted Arty with disgust, "you can almost always find a money trail with those who are trying to build up their religious organizations."

"Yeah, my dad said his friend Bill brings these big drawings of this magnificent cathedral with its pinnacles pointing to heaven where God is pictured above looking down with a smile... and they show this to the natives, and it really has got my dad upset about it all. My dad, of course, sees through the ploy, and it's interesting that my dad has commented from his letters last fall about some small thatched roofed little chapel... that I suppose some true believers are using for meetings down there ...because my dad has said they are Bible translators, and he is kinda friendly with them and thinks they have the good of the natives in mind. And he has said that some of the music and hymns that those Bible translators have taught the natives has given them more peace and happiness and tranquility than their noisy and depressing drum beating and chants...."

"That's interesting," Bob commented as he was listening on, "maybe God is using those Bible translators to soften your dad up a little?"

"Well, they call upon my dad's medical help every once in a while, and so they show a lot of respect for my dad's work, so that's good," Craig added.

"And it just shows you," Bob continued, "how the New Testament's description of those small, house type churches and meeting places seems to emphasize a better way for reaching out than building huge cathedrals... and it keeps leaders from getting caught up in being celebrities or trying to raise money to build some edifice to their glory... I mean big churches might work okay in big corporate America where people are impressed with buildings and big business type things, but not in a jungle of thatched roofed houses and poverty," Bob declared.

"I'll tell you though, Bob," Craig observed, "it's a lot like my aunt's home group, it was appealing to me...and that Creation Bible

Over the Big Pond

study wasn't intimidating to me like walking into some big impersonal church and just getting all emotional over some 'hyped up' musical performance, or a 'feel good' 30 minute 'do good' type pep-talk, like I used to go to."

Arty smiled at Craig's honest humor and replied, "Just shows you again how the New Testament model wasn't just an accident, and kept Christians away from exalting buildings and impressive and dramatic speakers."

"Yeah, Arty," Bob added, "I think it was the church in Rome that was one of the first ones to get involved in a big building project that led to Bishops and Cardinals and then the 'Pope' and a big counterfeit Christian religion. We read in the New Testament about the house churches, and we in America think, Oh, poor Christians, if they would have had more money in those early days they could have built big mega-churches, not even realizing that God had presented a better plan. But, oh well, I guess it's a lot like home schooling...there are some folks who will never give it any credit for being any good, because the traditional school building is thought of as the only way to have 'school', just like the

The Case of the skeptic Doctor

traditional church building is the only way to have church."

"Yep... score one more for the traditions," Arty murmured while watching the distant sky in front of them.

The hours passed quickly over the miles of water that lay below them, as the 3 young men continued their discussion of a wide range of topics until at last the Yucatan Peninsula came into view.

"We'll fly along the coast until we get down to Costa Rica and there re-fuel," Bob explained. In an hour they landed in San Jose, Costa Rica, and refueled.

Once in the air again, the trio continued their journey south, and it was dusk when they arrived at Bogata, Colombia. Bob recognized the high peaks around the city, and after getting landing instructions proceeded to bring the plane down and landed, and then they taxied to the outskirts of the field, and after a visit from customs officials they settled down for the much needed night of rest. Bob fixed supper while Arty and Craig looked over the plane and had it fueled up by a fuel truck. They tried to talk a bit

Over the Big Pond

with the friendly driver of the truck, but the language barrier made it difficult. After dinner Arty played some hymns on his guitar until the tired trio retired for the night.

Bob's final words were, "Tomorrow night it might not be so easy to find a place to land. I have a feeling we'll be flying over miles and miles of jungle looking for a landing strip somewhere."

"Really," Craig said with an inquisitive expression on his face.

Chapter 7

Heavy Devastation

The next morning their flight carried them south down the slopes of the northern Andes, and they soon entered into what seemed to be endless miles of jungle. At last they began to see the tributaries that fed the Amazon River coming down out of the Andes Mountains in western Brazil. As Arty pointed west he said, "The rivers that feed the Amazon Basin start about 75 miles from the Pacific Ocean in Peru where there is snow melt from the Andes Mountains even in this tropical climate."

"My dad said the Amazon has over a thousand smaller tributaries emptying into it that gives it more water flow than any other river in the world where it dumps into the Atlantic near the equator. He said its flow is greater than the

The Case of the Skeptic Doctor

Mississippi and the Nile and Yangtze rivers combined," Craig said and then added, "And, at its mouth, the Amazon River is nearly 60 miles wide, and 2000 miles from the ocean it is still 2 miles wide...so the only way to cross it, other than flying over it, is by boat. So there's an endless number of boats and ships of all kinds from little native canoes and outriggers to ocean-going barges, always going about on those vast waterways."

Arty was studying the map, "Looks like we've got a couple hours of flying...didn't you say your dad's compound was in this region?" he questioned pointing to the spot on the map.

"Yep, that's it, right there in the area where the Rio Negro and the Rio Branco divide," Craig answered.

"Well," Arty said thinking outloud, "if we can't use your dad's landing strip, that is if it's flooded, I guess we might have to rent us some floats somewhere to attach to our plane and land on water...we've done that before."

Bob added his thoughts, "Or we could land downstream at some airport and then rent a boat of some kind."

Heavy Devastation

"That's a thought, but it would take days of water travels, and we might need to fly in and out to carry med supplies or to do some emergency evacuation, so we might need the plane," Arty replied wondering.

"My dad says there are thousands of miles of navigable rivers with hundreds of tribes folks they could help with a hospital boat. It's always been his wish to have a floating clinic of some kind," Craig commented.

"When we get there, let's just fly in and take a closer look, and it may conserve cost and fuel to fly down to Manaus, looks like the closest big city, and rent some floats...maybe there will be some available down there, and it's about 200 miles, or an hour and a half or so from here flight time...it may save time just using Old Gabe," Bob speculated.

"That's the city my dad flies his Beechcraft down to every month," Craig added.

"But could that airport in Manaus be flooded?" the younger brother wondered.

"Hmm...could be, but that's a major city."

"I'd like to check at the post office there in Manaus anyway," Craig said, "that's where

The Case of the Skeptic Doctor

my dad gets and sends his mail...my mom was wondering if maybe some of her letters to dad are still at the post office in Manaus unable to be picked up by dad because of the flooding."

"Sure thing," Bob replied.

"Dad said in the last letter I got from him, about 3 months ago, that most of the garden plots of the villagers are flooded, and the corn and yams and cassava that they depend on for food is lost. Those natives get a lot of their food from hunting and fishing, too, but they put out gardens, and after a while the constant rains down here wash out all the nutrients in the soil, and so the villagers move on to another location and clear the forest underbrush and use that fertile soil under those trees for a few seasons until the soil gets depleted again in time, and then they move on again," Craig explained and then added, "In Dad's last letter he said his landing strip was partially under water, and that Bill Paris had flown his plane out before the landing field was completely flooded."

"Tell me more about this Bill Paris. Is he considered a missionary?" Arty said passing the time as they flew around the region.

Heavy Devastation

"Bill is an old friend of my dad's from high school who has kept in touch with my father, and has been working with dad some," Craig explained as they talked while they traversed over the seemingly endless miles of jungle forest.

"Bill and dad used to go flying a lot together in college, and Bill, like dad, is an amateur anthropologist, and he and dad used to fly to archeological digs in Africa and South America. They were both big on Evolution."

"So that's their connection," assented Bob. "That's going to make our job trying to reach your father even more difficult if Paris is down here."

"I think he's up in New York right now," Craig replied.

"Oh, good," Bob said sounding relieved.

Craig went on, "That's how my dad first became acquainted with the natives in this region. They flew down here, and the natives would show them caves that had ancient art on the walls...and so it intrigued my dad, and he wanted to do some archeological research, too. And years ago Bill Paris used to try to get us to

The Case of the Skeptic Doctor

join his church, back when I was a boy, and though his religion has a worldwide membership, my dad always said it seemed like a cult, and so we avoided it. Bill used to come over to our house with his little handout booklets that talked about some 'kingdom' we could become a part of if we joined their church," Craig said smiling sounding a little sarcastic, as he went on, "and then a couple years ago, Paris started asking my dad about his work down here, and Bill decided to join my father and help out with medical assisting, and do his 'missions work?' for his church on the side."

"Oh, so Bill's a doctor?" Arty asked.

"No, he's a medical assistant...Bill's an interesting guy. He bounced around in a lot of jobs after high school. He worked in a jewelry shop for a while but got fired when they kept losing inventory from their store, and the owner said Bill wasn't diligent enough in watching over things when he displayed jewelry to customers like diamond rings that would disappear now and then, and so the owner let him go. After that Bill enrolled at the same college as my dad, and they used to get pretty excited about studying

Evolution. It was the big thing in those days. After college Bill did some training as a medical assistant in a clinic over in Rochester, New York, and he ended up coming down here to assist dad in his medical work," Craig said, and then added, "But when he came down he started taking his little religious booklets around to the natives saying he was doing 'missionary' work, and this kinda perturbed my dad, but what could he say...but it doesn't sound like Bill Paris has been real dependable for my dad." Craig went on, "He stays a few weeks and then makes excuses for going back to the states and wants to borrow my dad's plane, and he says he'll have FAA required maintenance work done on the plane back in the States. But my dad's been getting more disgusted with Bill's lack of responsibility, and lately dad said he's been looking for someone more dependable to replace him. I hope I can take over for Paris."

"Sounds like your dad would be better off without him around," Bob commented.

"Yeah, I think Bill's on one of his maintenance trips back north," Craig said rolling his eyes. "I hope so anyway... I think Bill's religion gets my dad confused and thinking that all religions are the same, just different dreamed-up theological ideas and religious duties that people get tangled up in."

"Well, that's what most religions are," Bob said in a matter-of-fact tone.

"But what about med school? Are you going to quit med school and work with your dad?" Arty put in the thought.

"I may take a break from school for a while. My dad is an outstanding surgeon, and I'm hoping to learn from him in an apprenticeship or internship style. Dad says he can train me in about 6 months time to learn what most med students spend years of wasted expensive college time learning. You know years ago before schools became big business, most doctors used to train under a good physician instead of classes with so-called certified instructors. The old way was just as good," Craig offered.

"We know what you mean," Arty continued. "Being home schooled, we know lots of guys and girls who have really excelled academically, and even a couple brothers who got perfect scores on their SAT's whose mother that taught them was not even a high school graduate. The big argument from the unionized teachers has always been that parents aren't 'qualified' to teach their own, and over and over again that's being proven untrue. And not that academics has to be the only focus of home schooling either, sometimes it's other talents that need to be emphasized like artistic skills, or music skills, or mechanics skills, or business skills."

"Yeah, you met Rusty, dad's chief technician," Bob interjected. "He's not even a certified tech, but dad says he's got more knowledge and experience than most of the airplane tech school instructors do, though the airlines won't hire him as an airplane technician because he's not certified."

"Oh, really!" Craig shook his head.

"Yeah, our brother Josh is training under Rusty in aircraft technology, but Josh can't get certified either unless he can show he got his training at some tech school," Arty continued the point and then said, "Somehow those schools get in control in about every field, and even with Christian things, like, you know, Craig, some of the most renowned and respected Bible teachers

The Case of the Skeptic Doctor

and preachers of the past, like D.L. Moody and Charles Spurgeon, were self-taught and never even went to Bible school or Seminary, but now it's only the graduates from the Bible schools that are said to be 'qualified' to lead."

"Interesting...sounds like another tradition getting in there," Craig observed.

Arty nodded being encouraged with Craig's growing discernment.

"Yep," Arty said, "the New Testament teaches that Churches were to select their leaders and teachers from among their own older men, where their character, Bible knowledge and spiritual insight, faith, and experience was known by all the members...but again, somehow, Bible schools have been elevated above what Paul taught and the so-called 'professionally trained' or 'certified' pastors are presented as being, for the most part the only ones able to lead Christians. We even know of a Creation scientist who has edited an outstanding commentary Bible, that wouldn't be considered 'qualified' to be a pastor because he hasn't graduated from a Bible college."

"Really!" Craig sounded incredulous.

"Yep, most churches are just like classrooms where folks are expected to sit and listen and study their whole lives, but are never expected to graduate or to participate in 'exhorting one another', or even going out and starting something new of their own, by 'teaching others also' as Paul directed, and as they did in the Early Church days....the tradition of our day has made ministry a lot more difficult than God intended it to be."

Just then Bob spoke up glancing out his side window at two converging rivers, "Looks like we're in your father's region."

Looking below they observed deep flooding, and as they surveyed scenery, they flew over at least a dozen groups of tribal folks huddled together in spots of higher rolling ground...all looked to be in bad straits. At last they saw what appeared to be Dr. Armstrong's site, as Arty and Craig searched the area with binoculars, and Arty spotted what looked to be the compound to the south east. "Bank about ten degrees east, Bob. I think I see it."

"Roger," Bob said turning the yoke slightly as Craig pointed his binoculars in the same direction, but as they circled around they could see no landing strip. There were many houses at the edge of those rivers built up on stilts.

"Dad said in one of his letters that a lot of them live in houses built on those stilts out in the river for safety. Dad said a medical boat or ship of some kind would be handy in helping those villages built on stilts like that," Craig said describing their future hopes.

After a while of useless search for a landing sight, they decided to drop some of their supplies by parachute down to Craig's father's compound, and then fly to Manaus and see if they could rent some floats for their plane. Craig wrote a note and put it in with the supplies they dropped telling his father of their plans. Dropping down close to the tree tops they came gliding over the compound seeing Dr. Armstrong amidst a crowd of native families waving to them in curiosity and gratitude.

Heading south in a little over an hour, following the Amazon River they spotted the town of Manaus. Arty radioed the airport tower, and after a moments silence, he was relieved to

Heavy Devastation

hear a voice replying in broken yet understandable English giving them the okay and instructions for landing. Bob lined up with the strip and skillfully brought Old Gabe down for a smooth landing.

Arty spoke out, "There's an old Gooney bird over there... maybe it had some floats on it?".

The Case of the Skeptic Doctor

They taxied to what was a rather basic metal building terminal, with a windowed control room on top and with a beacon light that appeared to have only one of its rotating lights working. Bob scanned the lot while they taxied to the terminal hoping to see some floats among the hulks of old airplanes and other related paraphernalia scattered among the weeds. Arty spoke out, "There's an old Gooney bird over there... maybe it had some floats on it?"

"Gooney Bird?" Craig said wondering.

"Yeah, that's what they used to call these DC3's back in the war, and a lot of these countries down here in South America acquired these old war surplus DC'3s, or C47's transports that were made from DC'3s, and remodeled them and put seats in them to start up their airline companies after the war," Arty explained.

Their quest to find some pontoons or floats for Old Gabe ended with disappointment as they were informed that if there were ever any around they had long ago been put to use by the many sea-planes in the Amazon region. While the perplexed aviators sat down for some dinner in Old Gabe, they bantered over what their options now were for getting into Dr. Armstrong's compound.

"We might be able to land air-craft carrier style on the short end of your father's grass runway there that's not flooded, but it will be impossible to take off again until the water recedes from the full length of it," Arty mentioned.

Craig was wondering what Arty meant by air-craft carrier style, but then Craig said, "They are coming into a more dry season down here, but it still could be a few weeks before the full runway can be used I'm sure," he said offering his suggestions.

Bob looked to Craig as if he was weighing his suggestion, but then Craig still being curious said, "What's an air-craft carrier style landing anyway?"

"Oh," Arty smiled, "when they land on carriers, they catch the plane on the deck runway with cables stretched across it that are lifted to catch a tail hook on the landing plane, and the cables absorb the forward thrust of the plane and slow it down suddenly...and I was thinking if your dad's natives could straw a lot of jungle vines across the runway, our landing gear would plow into them, but they would slow our plane considerably."

Bob rolled his eyes with an amusing grin at what he thought was his brother's lame-brain idea and said, "Yeah, and we might just flip over, too, after all those vines pack against our wheels, or our nose might tilt forward enough to dig a canal down the runway," he laughed.

"It was just an idea," Arty replied realizing he hadn't thought it through enough, and then said, "But right now we have a plane full of emergency supplies that need to be dropped to aid those many stranded villagers."

"That sounds like our first project," Bob agreed and added, "I say we refuel and then bunk down here in Old Gabe tonight, and at the break of day we fly down into the region by Dr. Armstrong's and see where the supplies appear to be most needed, and parachute drop them down from our cargo bay, and then we'll see what's next."

To that the aviators were in agreement, as Bob's plan sounded like the best next move.

Chapter 8

A Daring Parachute Rescue

As they circled around the jungle region just beyond Dr. Armstrong's compound, they spotted a couple dozen village make-shift camps on higher ground. And after a couple of "missed" parachute drops that glided over the camps into the nearby swamps, the fellas were getting their timing down better with dropping supplies. They would level out a few hundred feet above the tree tops, high enough to allow the parachutes to open, and Bob would estimate the distance from the camps as best he could, and then call back on the intercom for Craig and Arty to "heave" the load with its attached parachute out the back door. A thin twine line hooked to the parachute ripcord and the other end attached to the plane would pull out the parachute ripcord

The Case of the Skeptic Doctor

when the bundle reached a hundred feet below the plane, and then the ripcord would pull open the chute allowing the bundle to glide freely and fall into the camp sight below. Finally they were getting their timing and flight speed adjusted perfectly to drop the supplies safely right beside the people gathered below. Each bundle had enough food to last around a month for a group of 50 or so. Each bundle also had blankets and tents and cooking pots and some first aid med supplies which they feared the tribes folks might not be able to understand how to use, but the food was the most important item to them. By mid-afternoon they had dropped most of their supplies, and had gotten some to all the camps they could find flying over Dr. Armstong's compound for one last pass over before heading east back to Manaus. They wished there was some way to communicate with him, but with his plane being gone there was no radio available to talk back and forth. They had not gone far when suddenly, out of the corner of his binoculars, Arty spotted what looked to be a tiny camp.

"Hold up a minute, Bob," Arty announced with alarm staring at the spot below. "I thought I saw smoke from a small campfire and what looked to be a man laying on the ground beside it. I'll keep the glasses on the spot while you circle back," Arty said as Bob banked the plane.

"Yeah, I see the smoke coming up in a clearing in the middle of those trees," Craig said looking through his set of binoculars. There was a small raised area not more than an acre or so in size surrounded by swampy flood waters all the way around. Bob flew the plane in a large arc around and then flew back diving towards the same spot dropping his speed to what seemed like a crawl.

"There he is! I see him," Craig declared followed by Arty, "Yeah, I've got him too!" Then Craig continued, "Looks like a youth...I would say."

"Yeah...I agree, and he looks either sick or just emaciated from hunger and not able to even sit up," followed Arty's comments. "How long has this flooding been going on?"

"Several months," was Craig's dire assessment.

"He could be at a point of death...we've

The Case of the Skeptic Doctor

got to do something," Arty said, moved by the plight of the lad.

"But what!" Craig said with passion. "Should we try to drop him something?"

"He doesn't appear to be in any condition to help himself," Arty said as he started reaching for his pilot's parachute.

"What are you doing?" Bob demanded of his impulsive brother.

"I thought I might try a little sky-diving."

"Very funny," Bob said frowning.

"Well, we've got to do something! He's miles away from all those village camps...we can drop our emergency bundle first, and then I'll jump on the second approach with one of our pilot survival packs and an inflatable raft that I can inflate if I land in the water, and hang on to the raft if I need it...I mean if I overshoot the island and land far out in deep water."

"It's a crazy risk, putting it mildly," Bob peeved, "I mean that little raised area is not more than fifty yards wide! It would take miraculous accuracy to jump at the right moment to land you on it."

"Well, you've been calling 'em all day,

A Daring Parachute Rescue

and those supplies are landing close to the exact spot, and so let's try to hit it with our emergency supply pack, and if we are successful, then maybe that will be a sign I'm to give it a try...and besides, if I miss, it might not be a bad thing anyway, because I've got the raft, and I can inflate it, climb into it and then paddle back to the island," Arty said sounding positive.

Bob didn't like the sound of putting his brother into such a risky situation, but he agreed to at least see if they could drop the emergency pack on the tiny spot below. Craig stood ready at the bay doors to toss out the smaller pack as Bob circled around and began his approach. Bob concentrated tensely as they neared the target, and then calling out on the intercom at what he thought was the precise moment..."Let her fly!"

Out it went, and then seconds later the chute opened, and the package began to glide down. Bob banked the plane, and they all gazed from the windows as seconds later Arty shouted with joy, "**Bullseye!**"

Craig joined in with a cheer, but then said, "That was easy, but you're worth a lot more than a bundle of blankets and beans."

The Case of the Skeptic Doctor

"Not much more," Arty mumbled, "but the boy hasn't hardly stirred...we've got to do more," he said as he contemplated a jump.

Then Bob said, "What are you going to do once down there?"

"I don't know...I suppose take the boy in the raft to Dr. Armstrong's compound to get him looked after...I'll have to assess his condition," Arty replied.

"Well, let me get the coordinates so you can know exactly which way to navigate your life raft...do you still have that pocket compass Gramps gave you?" Bob said as he lined the plane up in the direction of Armstrong's compound.

"Yep, right here," Arty said tapping his pocket.

As Bob flew over the tiny island the boy was stranded on, he determined the direction to the clinic. "Looks like exactly due west," Bob said studying the plane's compass and bearing. "And I would estimate you'll be about 10 miles from the clinic, and about the same to any of the stranded villagers."

"Okay, that makes it easy," Arty said as

A Daring Parachute Rescue

he headed back to the tail of the plane to get ready for his jump.

Moments later Bob could feel the tenseness of the situation as Arty with his pilot's chute on and the life raft rolled up tightly around the paddles, and gear tucked under his arm, knowing that when his chute opened there would follow a sudden jerk on his straps, and the inflatable raft and its contents would want to dislodge from his grip, so he held it tightly. Slowly Bob navigated for the second approach, while Arty stood ready to leap from the plane.

Sweat rolled down Bob's forehead as he tried his hardest to calculate the exact jumping off point, but at last he felt it was the right time.

"Jump!" Bob shouted over the intercom, and seconds later out the side window he saw his brother descending towards the target.

One, two, three seconds later his chute opened slowing his descent, and moments later Arty passed over the tops of some trees and plunked down perfectly at the water's edge.

"Phew!" Bob breathed a sigh of relief as he watched his brother come to his feet in knee deep water and start walking up on the island.

The Case of the Skeptic Doctor

"That was a miracle!" Craig declared as he climbed into the seat beside Bob.

"Amen," Bob whispered.

"Jump!" Bob shouted over the intercom, and seconds later out the side window he saw his brother descending towards the target.

A Daring Parachute Rescue

One last trip around Arty waved from below as he went over and kneeled down beside the stricken youth.

He was weak and sick from exposure and in desperate need! He could barely raise his head. He had a bad gash in his shin above his ankle that had quit bleeding, but it was swelling up! Arty only hoped it wasn't badly infected. Arty went to open the bundle of supplies to look for some topical antiseptic, some fresh water, and some cans of soup. He only wished he had some penicillin, but they had dropped it all to Dr. Armstrong's clinic on their last pass.

Opening a can of soup he poured it into a small pan and set it on the coals for warming. There was a small pile of sticks the boy must have collected before he grew weaker, and had laid within his reach to put on the fire.

Bob and Craig circled around for one last fly over, while Arty attended his weary patient.

"I guess I could try jumping and parachuting down to my dad's compound," Craig said in a reluctant tone thinking about how easy Arty made it look.

Bob stared at Craig to see if he was serious, "Have you ever tried jumping or had any training with it?"

"No, afraid not. About the last thing I remember jumping off was the back roof of my father's shed trying to get away from some nasty hornets I uncovered when tearing off shingles when I was about thirteen," Craig laughed.

"How'd you land? Any twisted ankles?"

"No, I just bent my knees to absorb the impact and rolled forward in a ball all in one motion."

"Well, believe it or not, that's part of the technique for landing with a parachute jump, I mean legs bending at the knees to absorb the initial impact and then tumbling forward...some people have a natural ability to protect themselves in a fall, while others stiffen up and end up getting injured," Bob replied.

Craig was listening, and the thought came to him, "So... are you thinking it might not be that difficult to try 'dropping in' on my father?"

Bob smiled at Craig's pun and then said, "Well, at least he could fix you up if you break a leg," Bob added glancing back over with a grin.

A Daring Parachute Rescue

"It doesn't sound too risky...I might be up for it if nothing else comes along," Craig said as Bob pointed the plane in the direction of Manaus...it was getting late in the afternoon.

While Bob and Craig flew back to the airport, Arty was busy attending his patient and was surprised to hear the boy say a few words in English.

The nourishing soup seemed to revive the youth a little, and Arty stuffed a rolled up sleeping bag under his neck and shoulders and was trying to console the boy who appeared to be twelve or thirteen. "How did you end up away from your tribe?" Arty asked while spooning him sips of soup.

"About two moons ago was sent on my warriors quest for manhood that all young boys go through at my age, and after three days was caught in terrible storm and hurt my leg when running to safe place. All I had was two pots of cassava beans and my warriors bow and hand axe, but no way to escape this small island after heavy rain, and so after one week grow very hungry, and become weaker and weaker and thought I must soon die, and so prayed that God would save me. Then I had dream of a white angel coming down and helping me, and when I looked up today and saw you falling from the sky with white sheet above you, I knew God had heard my cry."

"Well, I'm no angel, that's for sure," Arty confided, "but maybe I can help you get better." And then said, "My name is Arr...ty," he said slowly saying it and pointing to himself...what is your name he asked pointing to the lad.

"I be Myko,"

Arty smiled at his new friend, a pleasant looking youth with dark olive brown skin and soft brown eyes, wearing long pants made of what looked to be deer or goat skin, and a loose white shirt made of cotton. He was surprisingly well covered compared to the way most natives in the wild are dressed. Arty was wondering if his people had been visited by missionaries or if they were familiar with Dr. Armstrong, because obviously some religious group had been among them for him to be able to speak English, and to be dressed so well and with a shirt on. In a while, as the boy seemed to gain some slight strength, Arty inquired of him in a kind tone of voice,

A Daring Parachute Rescue

"How did you learn white man's tongue?"

"First white man come and teach school for childrens, where Myko learn to speak white man's tongue and read white man's book."

"Huh," Arty thought with surprise as the boy continued slowly.

"Then great white man come with book of mighty kingdom pictures, and teach my people of great kingdom to be ours if we give diamonds to build great mighty house for God to live in and come to be with us for 1000 years."

"Oh, boy," Arty mumbled to himself with a sigh, "..sounds like Paris' doings... seems he's getting back in the jewelry business," he sarcastically thought to himself as he asked the boy some more questions, seeing he seemed to want to talk.

"Diamonds, where do you get diamonds?"

"Dig diamonds from deep pit not far from village," Myko said pointing west, "and give to great white teacher, and he take to his Priests far away so he can come and build great temple for people to live with God many thousand years."

"Do you know great white man's name?"

The Case of the Skeptic Doctor

Arty inquired.

"His name be...Parr...ess."

"Bill Paris no doubt," Arty thought to himself."Do you know Dr. Armstrong?" Arty asked.

"Yes, we go to Armstrong to get medicines once, twice, but white man Parr...ess, say he give medicine that not good for poor natives...so we no more go to Dr. Armstrong," the boy said.

"That's strange," Arty thought to himself, "I wonder what Paris is up to," but from what Craig had told them about Bill Paris, Arty was able to put two and two together. Thinking this was probably the reason for Bill's frequent trips back to the states, he was probably cashing in those diamonds he was getting from this boy's tribe. Arty then asked, "How often does great white man come and get diamonds?"

"Once or twice every new moon."

"Every couple weeks," Arty figured giving him time about every month to fly back north in Armstrong's plane to do his maintenance work," Arty thought being perturbed with the scheme.

A Daring Parachute Rescue

Arty could see the boy was getting weary from talking and noticing the sun setting he said, "You lay back now and sleep, and I'll keep watch in the dark."

Then the boy said, "Keep fire burning to scare off wild beasts...wild beasts come."

"Okay, I will," Arty said as he laid a couple of broken sticks on the fire and set to work putting up a small tent, and fixing himself a little dinner...the boy was soon sound asleep.

Though Arty knew the fire would keep away most predators, it would also be a beacon light to attract others, so he unrolled the raft and got out grandpa's old double barrel shotgun that he had laid between the paddles in the bundle. The shotgun, that he wasn't even sure would be of any real use, was now a welcome companion in the darkness, and he could now see how the Lord had led gramps to give it to him, and he had folded it in with the life raft oars and his fishing pole. It was a twelve gauge double barreled shotgun that would pack a good wallop on any creature that might venture to step foot out of the swamp onto their little island refuge. He only wished he had some deer slugs in his pocket

The Case of the Skeptic Doctor

instead of the few shot loaded shells...they would have to do.

Arty kept the fire blazing until about midnight when he dozed off, but was startled by what was sounding like some creature sloshing in the water right off the shore of the island. The fire had dwindled to a mere bed of coals giving no light as the menacing sound in the water grew louder. Arty could feel his heart pounding as he felt under his bedroll for his flashlight. At last grasping it in one hand and the shotgun in the other, he went towards the water's edge casting the beam around but saw nothing except what appeared to be water turbulence stirred up by something below the surface. Then suddenly he was alarmed to realize that he couldn't hold the light and at the same time grip and fire his shotgun, and while he studied as how to do both at the same time, suddenly in front of him two eyes raised up above the water's surface and, what looked to be the long snout of a crocodile in front of them. Knowing those formidable creatures often grow to be of immense size and that once on land they can race ahead faster than a man can run, Arty's instinct was to run to their campsite and grab the boy's hand ax to prepare for some kind of "hand to snout" combat, but while running to camp he quickly dismissed the foolish thought of that.

Instead, once back at camp, he saw the thin cords that held together his bundled-up life raft and quickly opening it and laying his long handled flash light next to, and underneath his shotgun barrel he carefully lashed the light snugly under the double barrels of the gun and tied it. Raising it, and sighting down the gun the flashlight cast its beam in the same precise direction as the aim of the shotgun. "Good!" he thought. Working his way back now silently as possible through the wet grass and gazing over the tops of the weeds, there at the water's edge lay the fiery eyes of the beast poised to spring at him the instant Arty came close enough to grab. Arty realized his only hope of dispatching the brute would be to give those eyes a blast from his gun in hopes of blinding the ferocious creature. Quietly pulling back the hammer with his thumb and then slowly raising the gun so as not to startle the brute into action, and casting the beam of the light, the red glowing eyes came

The Case of the Skeptic Doctor

into view.

Carefully squeezing the trigger the gun responded with an ear splitting "**boom!**", and instantly the giant lizard let out a horrific bellowing grunt followed by moaning and roaring all at the same time writhing in the muddy water's edge in pain. The shot had rendered the beast sightless, but Arty kept the second barrel ready for action in the event the huge reptile should come bounding out of the water towards him, but to his relief he could see the serrated tail flailing wildly in a wake of churning water heading through the lagoon back into the wooded area in the distance.

"Phew! That was close!" Arty gasped, "and now I know why gramps had given me shot instead of slugs...the shot was perfect for blinding that beast," he thought to himself in thankfulness as he cast the gun and beam of light around the water's edge in the vicinity of the enraged reptile, knowing that such often hunted in packs. But at last after a careful survey of the bank, he was satisfied that it was a lone assailant, and finally after a good half hour's search of the waterline, he went back to the camp find-

A Daring Parachute Rescue

ing Myko still in a deep sleep. Piling a good supply of sticks on the fire this time, it was soon in a blaze, and though the fire gave a greater sense of security, Arty found it impossible to sleep, and he could only doze off for a few minutes before time and again waking with a start.

Keenly he listened for any more night visitors, and wished for the daylight more than anyone who ever hoped for the morning. Finally though weary from no sleep, the morning began to brighten, and as it grew lighter Arty noticed the boy stirring, and so he opened a couple cans of beef stew and set them by the glowing coals for breakfast. As he wondered if the boy would be feeling well enough for traveling that day in their inflated raft, it mattered not however far they could get. Arty felt it would be much safer and easier than spending another night helplessly perched on their tiny island prison laying awake listening for some hideous intruder to pay them a visit.

Chapter 9

Through the Swamp

Arty was surprised to find Myko feeling much better when he awoke, and he was even able to sit up and talk and seemed to be in more amiable spirits. After some breakfast Myko tried to stand, but could only walk with a painful limp, and was pointing over to the life raft that Arty just inflated.

"Boat," he said.

"Yes...go on water to Dr. Armstrong's" Arty posed the idea to the boy pointing in the general direction.

He nodded and said, "Sound much good."

Arty thought there was no time to be wasted, their canned food and fresh water in the survival pack would last for only a week at the

The Case of the Skeptic Doctor

most; and wanting the boy to get some antibiotics into his system, Arty knew they had better get going. Loading up the raft they were soon on their way, but Arty was annoyed by the sluggish travel of their little dinky boat; the only positive thing about it was that being so small it could be easily maneuvered around the endless profusion of trees and vines. The one big concern was to be on the alert for thorn trees which were numerous in those parts. One puncture could spell sure disaster. But then Arty comforted himself when he thought the Lord is as much the Lord of the swamp as He is Lord of the sky...He will keep us safe.

As they paddled around what seemed to be an endless entanglement of trees, Myko handled an oar on one side in back and Arty in front rowing on the other side. At one point Myko reached forward to grasp Arty's arm, which amused Arty as he looked to the boy, and then he realized that the boy wasn't sure Arty was a real man and was still wondering if Arty may be an angel dropped from heaven. Arty at first thought of trying to explain again that he was just a man, but then he thought there might

Through the Swamp

be some advantage in leaving things alone; the boy might hold him in greater respect. Arty could sense the boy had appreciative feelings towards him, and Arty, in turn, was impressed with the boy's gentle character. He hoped he could minister to his spiritual needs as well as his health needs.

Twisting and turning they slowly worked their way west through the profusion of dense undergrowth, and the canopy of tall leafed trees above made it impossible at times to see the sun. And so, time and again, Arty would produce his compass to make sure they were going the right direction, and several times he realized his hunch was right, that they had gotten twisted around and were going the wrong way. Oh how valuable that little hiker's compass was proving to be, that was again grandpa's idea.

They stopped once for a brief lunch of canned rations and then diligently proceeded on until late in the day when it was growing dim under the dense overgrowth when suddenly, gasping with fright, the boy pointed to something in the tree limbs in front of them. Darting his eyes towards the same spot, Arty was shocked to see an enormous anaconda snake dropping down from the limbs above ready to grab him the next moment. All in one move Arty reached back for the shotgun that was near his side, cocked it, and in one swift instant, he raised it and blasted a volley of shot towards the creature's head! **"Boom!!"** The gun sounded, but they were so close the shot didn't have time to spread out, and Arty had missed! A frantic grab for the other trigger followed as Arty in the confusion sought to make a better aim, followed by another deafening **"Boom"** as the gun roared, this time hitting his mark as the dreadful serpent slithered down and disappeared into the water below.

"Phew!" Arty gasped turning to Myko who sat pale and stunned by what had just happened. Then Myko began looking at the shotgun with a strange admiration gazing up and down at it, and then motioned raising his hands pretending as if he was raising the gun and then with an expression of utmost fear he whispered, "boom!" Arty smiled and nodded wondering if it was possible that the lad had never seen or heard a gun before.

Through the Swamp

Grasping the gun Arty moved the lever that allowed him to open the breach and ejected the spent shotgun shells; then he loaded two more fresh ones, the last two, from his pocket and snapped the barrel up locking it in place thinking to himself, "Why didn't I bring more shells with me? I'm so dumb at times," he thought chastising himself for not bringing the full box of shells. The boy seemed to want to keep his distance from the firearm as the roar of it had given him more fright than the sight of that huge snake.

Arty was realizing that the trees around could be full of such hungry slimy serpents, as the flood waters had driven them from their holes in the ground into the limbs of the trees, and the prospects of sleeping under this treacherous canopy filled with such varmints did not sound very inviting as Arty looked for a place to try to stop; it was getting too dark to continue on. At last to his surprise they came out into a large lake or lagoon, and once out in the middle of it a good distance from any trees, Arty felt reasonably safe; they would try to rest there for the night.

As night closed in, the chants and calls

of the doleful night creatures filled the air, and as best he could, he told Myko to stay awake and keep watch while he got a couple hours of rest; and so they spent the night alternating a watch, being relieved to, at last, see the morning sky begin to brighten.

The next day Arty learned more of his new companion's homelife. Myko had a younger brother named Niko, his mother was well, and his father was one of the leading chiefs in their village of nearly two hundred. It sounded to Arty like a Bible translator was once among his people and had learned much of their language, and had taught him when Myko was younger and the other children how to speak a little English and read from the book of God. It gave Arty joy to hear that some self-sacrificing Christian had given his life to reach the poor needy natives of the region. He only hoped that Paris had not gotten them confused with this notion of a temple to build for God in the jungle and this fable that God would come and live with them for a thousand years in that temple.

While Arty and Myko continued on their perilous jungle voyage, Bob and Craig were

Through the Swamp

trying to discern their next move. They decided to go down along the river docks in Manaus and see if they could find a river boat of some sort to rent. They inquired around as best they could due to the language barrier, but at last were directed to a company that takes jungle tours from houseboat cruise type ships.

"There it is," Craig said pointing to the sign that read: **Adventura de Jungula.**

There tied along the wharf were three rather large houseboats, but there did not appear to be anyone around. The ships or houseboats seemed to be shut up and empty, but finally after looking around for someone, Bob noticed smoke coming out of a tin pipe from the roof of one of the boats. Bob called over, "Any one around?!" They waited a few seconds, and Bob was about to repeat his inquiry when an older gentleman with a Mexican type sombrero and a white shirt and pants appeared at the door in front of the walkway behind the ship's railing.

"Ola, Amigos," the thin mustached man called over to the dock to Bob and Craig.

"Is the owner around?" Bob asked.

"Si, Senor! I am the owner," he replied.

The Case of the Skeptic Doctor

"Are you taking any river outings?" Bob inquired.

"No, Senor, business too slow because of the flooding, no crew for ships, business very bad..very bad....must sell ships."

Bob glanced to Craig with a thought of interest, as Bob continued. "Can two men run ships?" Bob asked looking over the houseboat that appeared to be around 50 plus feet in length having a steering house or pilot's house in the front built above on the flat top roof of the boat.

"Run ship?" the Spanish accented man inquired not understanding. Then Bob pointed to himself and then to Craig and said, "Can dos men sail ship?"

"Oh, si, Senor, but with no cook, no house keeper, no safari guide, no musicians...then no business, senor," came the man's dismal assessment.

Bob realized the man thought they wanted the boat to use as an adventure tour boat...but then Craig understanding what Bob had in mind said, "We want to buy the boat... can we see inside?"

"Si, Senor...come I will show," the man

said motioning for them to cross over on the walkway to the ship.

There was an open deck in front where they stepped onboard with some white painted deck tables with chairs for 3 or 4 set around each of them. They followed the man from the open porch deck to the front door and entered. A stairway went up to their left to the roof and steering room above, and a short hallway was in front of them which the man led them down. The first door to the left was the kitchen with a bar counter top with 5 bar type stools up to it. In back was a cooking surface with a fire under it the smoke from which went up the pipe they had first noticed. There was a refrigerator and cabinets above and below the counter. The smell of fried bacon hung in the room. To the left in the kitchen were two booths for customers or tour guests to use instead of bar stools.

Going across the hall from the kitchen there was what appeared to be the captain's quarters which had a bed and dresser, an upholstered chair, and an adjoining bathroom with tub, much like a compact motel room. Returning to the hall, and walking towards the back of the ship were four more small rooms, two on each side of the hall. These were obviously for guests. Seeing these, Craig whispered to Bob, "This boat would work perfectly for a medical ship, and my father could use these rooms to see patients in!" Bob nodded liking the idea, too. The hall led to the back door that opened to a short open area about 15 feet wide and the same in depth extending to the rear of the boat, and to the right was a stairwell going down to the hold of the boat. Going below they came to the engine room first. They entered in, and the man reaching up turned a switch to a light bulb, showing what looked to be an ordinary truck motor of considerable size which was the ship's powerplant. On the air breather were the words *Ford Super* **v-8** which Bob liked the looks of as he whispered to Craig, "It's a Ford, we'll be able to get parts for it if we need em."

Craig nodded.

Next to the engine room was a good size storage room complete with shelving and with what appeared to be a 250 gallon fuel tank for the engine.

"That should run this thing for a long

Through the Swamp

time," Craig speculated.

Going out, on the other side below was a ship's crew quarters with bunk beds, some clothes closets, and another bathroom.

Going back up they looked over the ship for rot and wear and tear, and she looked to be in fairly good condition as they followed the railed walk along the side of the boat returning to the bow or front of the ship. Once again on the veranda they went to the front and looking up, the ship's name was on a sign under the pilot house in big letters.

- Rio Explorador -

"The River Explorer," Bob said, "sounds good to me! I wonder how much he wants for it?" They followed the man back to the kitchen which served as his office, too, having a desk over in the corner of the room. When Bob and Craig first heard the price the man was asking, they were fearful that something illegal was involved, because the price seemed lower than they expected. So Bob asked the man if he could show them the title deed for the craft. The man produced a title that seemed to be in order, having an official Brazilian seal on it, and then as

The Case of the Skeptic Doctor

Bob thought about it, he realized the reason the price was lower was because of the currency exchange rate. The American dollar was worth at least fifteen times the Brazilian currency, so that the $2,400 dollar asking price would yield the man what amounted to at least $36,000 dollars in Brazilian money, which seemed like a rather generous price to pay for the ship. So they offered the man $2,000, which he accepted.

    Bob and Craig talked it over briefly, and Craig had abut a twelve hundred dollars cash given to him by his mother as a gift from the Boston Clinic. Bob could see that Craig was disappointed that he didn't have enough to pay for the ship. It was stretching their savings, but Bob felt he could not pass up the opportunity. So Bob said, "Arty and I want to contribute to your medical work. Can we pay the difference?" At first Craig declined the offer, but then seeing how eagerly Bob wanted to give to the work, he at last yielded to his sincere and kind generosity. After agreeing on the price with the old man, the boys thought they should drive the boat just to be sure all was in good running order though the man assured them everything was.

Through the Swamp

"We take ride in river and fill up the gas tank," the man said.

"Fill up the gas tank?" Bob replied with a puzzled expression.

"Si Senor."

The three men went below to the engine room, and entering the man went to an electrical panel on the wall and pulled down on the lever. Bob assumed this was the battery hookup to the engine. Then the man went over and pushed a red button mounted on a post beside the engine, and a slow cranking sound came as the starter motor began to turn the engine; then the man began to pull on a knob which Bob assumed to be the choke as the engine instantly began to sputter and come to life, and was quickly running at a rather smooth idle. Bob was surprised at how easily it had started and how smoothly it ran. Then reaching over the man pulled over a lever engaging the engine to the controls above in the steering room.

"Come, Senors," he said smiling going out of the room and up the steps. Going out on the deck the man lifted the tie ropes off the posts that were holding the ship dockside. Going atop

The Case of the Skeptic Doctor

to the steering house the man turned the wheel that moved the rudder, and then reaching he pulled back on a lever engaging the prop, and then slowly increasing the throttle lever the engine below could be heard rising in pitch as the prop turned faster propelling the craft out into the open water. The man pointed to a strange looking flatboat in the distance. As they proceeded towards it, the purpose became clear, as they saw gasoline pumps on the flatboat and the words **Sun Oil Company** on a sign across the top of the roof of the boat. It was a floating filling station!

"Of course," Bob smiled over to Craig, "Most of the travel down here is on water! Why not a floating gas station."

Manaus was a refinery city, and big oil tankers came into the harbor there at the refineries, and so gas was cheap, and so for just a few dollars they filled the large fuel tank below from a pipe that ran above and was opened on the walkway on the main deck. A steady whistling sound could be heard as the fuel was funneled down the pipe to the tank below. Then the man said, "When whistle sound stops...then tank is

Through the Swamp

full."

They listened on, and at last it stopped whistling, and the nozzle was let off. The attendant was paid, and leaving the station Craig and Bob took turns in motoring around the river and got the hang of the boat's operations. It was very stable on the water and easily maneuvered by the steering wheel. Being at last satisfied that everything was in good order, they returned dockside and spent some time learning the finer details of the ship's operations. Then after paying the man and helping him move his household stuff from the boat to the one beside it, they took the keys to their newly acquired missions ship. The gentleman who sold them the boat was most accommodating in helping Bob and Craig to become familiar with the operation of the boat with everything from kitchen appliances to the boat's water system that operated off the ship's batteries when they were out on the river and couldn't plug in to local electricity. The engine's altenator, of course, charged up the batteries when the engine was running.

Bob and Craig then went by taxi to the airport which was only a few minutes away from

The Case of the Skeptic Doctor

the harbor, made arrangements to store their plane for a few weeks with airport personnel, and then they loaded into the taxi all the supplies they could gather from Old Gabe; and after several trips to the markets in town, they had their boat well stocked with plenty of food and other necessities to help the stranded tribes folks. It was noon the next day when the two were finally ready to venture on the river. There were extensive maps of the river in the steering room as Bob came above after starting the engine. Manning the wheel Craig smiled over to Bob, "Ready for some RIO EXPLORODOR?"

"Aye, Aye, El Cap-e-tan," Bob said saluting with a smile as Craig slid up the throttle lever, and the houseboat slowly moved out into the open waters.

Chapter 10

Journey Up the River

The current on the Amazon was not swift, but it was steady, and so for hours the Ford engine drove the little floating, soon to be, medical clinic up stream towards Doctor Armstrong's compound. It would take two long days to reach the region of Armstrong's clinic, but at last they began to enter the flooded region, and now they had to try to find a way to locate the compound. Travel was slow and tedious as there was much floating debris around, and so they had to be careful with either grounding their boat or damaging their propeller on a submerged log or entangling it in vines. Long poles were helpful in pushing debris away as Bob manned a pole and Craig steered from above. Thankfully the compound was not that deep into the forest just a ways back from the river's edge.

    Though it was unknown to Craig and Bob, Arty was in the same vicinity and was working his way desperately through the snarled undergrowth coming up to what he thought was the edge of the land where the Armstrong compound lay. Myko had now grown feverish and very sick; Arty feared his swollen lower leg was infected and antibiotics had to be given soon. Arty was almost sure they had reached the higher ground that the compound was on, but Myko couldn't walk now on the swollen leg. Arty didn't know what to do as he drew up toward the shore, but was gripped with fear when seeing in a tree warming itself in the morning sun was a jaguar stretched out on a limb. The hungry ferocious cat had to have anticipated making a quick meal out of the unsuspecting voyagers as soon as they ventured on land. It was a jaguar for sure; its spotted coat was unmistakable, and Arty knew those vicious predators had even been known to slay huge alligators in a one-on-one combat. Arty also knew those powerful felines were not hesitant to come at them swimming in the water. Slowly he began to back

Journey Up the River

paddle his little boat, and the beast seeing this rose to a crouching position ready to launch himself at them by leaping from the branch into the water. Just then Myko was arousing himself from a feverish nap, and raising himself to his side on his bed of blankets he saw in an instant the looming peril Arty's eyes were fixed on, as he looked in the same direction.

In an instant, Arty raising his arms high over his head trying to frighten the vicious animal, shouted a screechy roar at the beast. But it was nothing doing, as the fiery eyes just calmly glared back in return without a quiver in his body, as he looked to be ready to make a leap into the water in pursuit of his victims at any moment.

Myko called out in a weak voice, "Shoot big boom gun...scare!"

"It was worth the try," Arty thought to himself, though the jag was too far away for the shot to be effective, "but it may scare him away if it doesn't enrage him."

But Arty's greatest fear was that if he fired, it would leave him with only one loaded shell left, the thought of which made him uneasy at spending the shot, but there seemed to

The Case of the Skeptic Doctor

be no other choice; and so raising the shotgun he fired a blast toward the beast! **"Boom!"** the gun resounded over the water.

Instantly the leopard screamed with a snarling yell, and then jumped down and disappeared into the thick tall grasses.

Arty drew a deep sigh of relief for the time being, but now the fear of Myko's health lay heavy on his mind again, and how could they safely get to the compound on land, having now only one shotgun shell left? The thought was annoying to him! Why had he not better prepared himself, or why did he even waste that shell trying to scare that animal? Even though it achieved its purpose, it had left him nearly helpless with now only one shot left. It was useless to keep harboring such discouraging notions, but Arty was sure they had better not try to venture on land at least in that vicinity. Was the Armstrong compound in the woods nearby? If it was he hoped that his shot may have possibly been heard by some of them and sent them in response to their aid...that is, if he had not somehow gotten off his course and had passed beyond the clinic and they were now going farther to the west. It was a desperate situation especially for the lad; if the infection wasn't checked soon, it would most likely take his life. Being a good distance from the land, Arty knew his next wisest choice was to pray, and so bowing his head he sought the Lord's help.

But though the shot had not been heard by those at the Armstrong compound, it was heard by Bob as he was outfront using the long pole to push debris away from the front of their houseboat. Bob was certain he had heard a shot and not just from any kind of rifle or even a hand gun; it was obviously the deep throat boom of a shotgun blast. Was it from a jungle safari group? He doubted that...or did some of the tribes now have guns? Or could it possibly have been a shot from grandpa's double-barrel shotgun, and was Arty trying to signal them? Bob bounded up the steps to discuss it with Craig, and Craig replied he thought he heard it, too, but he also wondered if it was the boat's motor back-firing. Bob was sure they should investigate, and so that's what they decided to do. As Craig steered the boat to the left to circle around in the direction of the shot, Bob went back down to his post

The Case of the Skeptic Doctor

with pole in hand, and listened for a second signal, but it was not to be repeated. But turning the boat into more open waters they moved around the point of the island where they, too, thought the Armstrong clinic was located. As they came around the farthest reaches of the island in front of them there in the far distant water was a tiny speck of something in the midst of a large bay of flood waters. Bob signaled up to Craig pointing in the direction of the speck. Proceeding towards it in a few minutes the figure of a man sitting in a tiny skiff was apparent as they drew near. It soon became even more clear to Bob that it was, indeed, Arty's inflatable little bobber of a boat. Bob was flushed with excitement, and Arty seeing the approaching houseboat wasn't sure what to think...whoever it was, he thought, it was a welcome sight. Within minutes Arty stared with a most curious expression on his face not believing what he was seeing standing in the bow of the boat before him.

"Praise God! It's you, Bob! I can't believe it!" he exclaimed with a most relieved smile across his face.

"We heard your signal shot, and it

Journey Up the River

couldn't have come at a more perfect time! Another five minutes and we would have been long gone," Bob explained.

"It wasn't a signal, and, in fact, it was my next to last shell, and I've been condemning myself for the last twenty minutes for wasting it trying to scare a jaguar out of a tree!"

"Really!?" Bob retorted and then said marveling, "Are not our extremities God's opportunities."

"I guess God even uses what we think are blunders for His purposes," Arty reflected. But then turning his attention to his sick patient he said, "The boy is in serious trouble with an infection in his leg, and he's real weak."

Arty helped the staggering lad over towards the short ladder on the side of the house boat. Seeing this Bob swung open the gated railing above the steps, and reaching down the two of them helped the boy onboard.

"Let's take him in here," Bob motioned with his head toward the doorway, and once inside they turned to the captain's room and laid the boy on the bed.

Reaching down Bob felt the lad's head;

The Case of the Skeptic Doctor

it was hot with fever. "Let me go get Craig...he'll know what to do," Bob said.

"He needs some penicillin. Do you know if Craig has some?" Arty said glancing around the room.

"Don't know, I'll check."

Within minutes Craig was assessing the boy's condition and readily agreed that antibiotics were essential. "I'll redress this wound on his ankle and try to let out some of the infection," Craig said while going through his doctor's bag and finding what he was looking for. The wearied lad swallowed the strange white pills and then laid his head down, and closing his eyes he was soon in a sleep.

"Our first patient onboard our floating med clinic," Craig said looking at the young native. "This is what we bought this boat for, and the Lord is already putting it to use," he marveled. "But now we need our first miracle, too! He's got a dangerously high fever," Craig added as he put a cool cloth on the boy's forehead.

"Come on," Bob said to Arty, "I'll give you a quick tour of our medical boat, and with it getting dark out, how about we settle here for

Journey Up the River

the night?" he asked looking to Craig.

"Sure thing. A quiet night's rest would be the best thing for the lad."

"And me, too!" Arty said. "This little safari I've been on has been a little eventful! I'll tell you about it afterwhile."

Bob showed his brother through the ship, and then they tied up to a lone tree that was out in the middle of a large lagoon of flood water a good distance from any land. And after hearing Arty's tale of adventure with fighting snakes and crocodiles, they were glad to be a safe distance from further intruders. Bob was soon joined in the kitchen and was getting dinner together when Craig came in and said he was encouraged to see the lad in a deep restful sleep, and thought his fever was down some, and things were looking more hopeful. But as nightfall came they decided to douse the onboard lights and go about with dim candles, so that if there were any hostile natives in the region, the light would not give them away.

The night passed slowly, and Bob kept watch a good part of the time from the pilot house above on the ship. With the break of day, they studied the maps and plotted their course for the morning, hoping to reach Doctor Armstrong's clinic by noon, that is, if they were reading the maps correctly. About nine o'clock the lad roused out of his slumbers and soon found himself among friends. The boy took immediately to Doctor Craig, as he began to be called, and Bob and Arty could see the compassion and skill of the young doctor, as he cared for his patient.

The seemingly endless turns in the river and backed-up flood waters into inlets and coves made it difficult to ascertain their exact location on the maps; they would have to do the best they could and depend more on the mercy of God to guide them to their desired haven. But by mid afternoon the brothers feared they had gone beyond the location of the Armstrong compound, and they contemplated backtracking. Bob went below to discuss things with Craig and found that he had the lad sitting up and in good spirits. As Arty related their dilemma to Craig, the boy caught on to the problem and spoke up, "Myko see?"

"Of course," Arty thought, "He's familiar with this river region," he said.

"A little walk would help the circulation in his leg anyway," Craig affirmed as they helped the boy to his feet, and carefully they worked their way out on to the front porch of the ship.

The boy gazed up and down the river, and then he said shaking his head and pointing, "No, no, boat go that way!"

They had, indeed, overshot the location, and Arty motioned up to Bob at the helm that they should turn about, which Bob promptly did, and the boy with keen concentration studied the distant bank of the river, and then smiled nodding his head. Slowly they rounded a turn in the river, and then pointing to an inlet of water he said, "There be Dr. Armstrong's."

Emotional and surprised do not adequately describe the reaction when a few minutes later Dr. Armstrong's friends came into view at the distant shore. Soon the sight of the approaching houseboat brought many curious onlookers to the shores by the compound, and when the doctor himself arrived, he was overjoyed to see his son standing at the rail of the boat.

" Craig" he called over with a smile, and seconds later father and son greeted onshore, "as

The Case of the Skeptic Doctor

you know I have never been much of a man of prayer, but for weeks I have prayed God would somehow help these poor people, and when your plane came over our compound a few days ago and dropped those supplies I began to change my mind about there being a God who does answer prayer."

"I know what you mean, Father," Craig said glancing to Bob and Arty.

Bob and Arty wisely contained their joy in hearing those words from Craig's father, but rejoiced within to realize that God seemed to be already at work preparing the elder doctor to hear words of faith.

Craig showed his father onboard their floating clinic, and he seemed delighted as he made a short tour. The elder doctor was overjoyed that his son had joined him in his work and had even bought this useful ship as a floating clinic. It was all overwhelming to him, and he, of course, recognized the young lad, Myko, as being the son of the chieftain that they had had a strange falling out with a year or so before. Craig insisted that his father take a look at the boy, and the elder doctor was satisfied that

Journey Up the River

his son had treated the affliction correctly, and was confident of his speedy recovery. Later that afternoon, after many curious and happy visitors from the Armstrong compound had toured the "Angel boat" as they began to call it, they all went over to the compound for a feast of yams and ham that the natives had prepared from a wild pig they had caught and roasted, and some fish from the river. It was a happy reunion though it was visited with sorrow from the aged doctor when he realized his brother Lee had passed on in an untimely way from a heart attack just a few months before. Craig shared of his visits to his brother's widow's place and told how Lydia had sent him down with Bob and Arty to report the sad news of his brother's passing and to try to help out.

"You know, I had just written a letter to my brother apologizing to him for how obstinate I had been in receiving his thoughts on Creation and his religion," the older doctor began to confess, "but then the rains came and the flooding, and I still have the letter here in a book he gave me some years ago on the Genesis flood. I had been reading it, and thought of it as amusing at first until one day I went with Myko's tribes folks to that old abandoned diamond pit or mine that they wanted to show me. And you know I'm an amateur geologist, and I was standing in that pit and looking at the limestone strata in front of me and noticed how they were not straight across horizontally as one would expect, but that they turned upward as if they were thrown upward somehow, and then the explanation from that book jumped into my mind. It said that the same day the rains came that the 'fountains of the great deep were broken up or burst open,' as that book said quoting Genesis, and I stood there looking at the walls of the pit and I said to myself...could it have possibly been true? I realized at that moment that the Bible's explanation for the geological structuring was more logical than the confusing explanations I had been taught for years by Evolution theorists, and I've been more intrigued with Creation science ever since that day."

Bob and Arty and Craig could hardly believe what they were hearing. It seemed to be an answer to prayer and clear evidence that God was at work preparing the elder doctor to be open

Journey Up the River

to further words of even deeper truth. Was God at work reconciling this skeptic doctor to Himself? The days and discussions ahead would be most revealing as the trio began to pray more earnestly for the elder man and his needy tribes folk.

Chapter 11

Reunion

The days that followed brought joy at the Armstrong compound, and the food supplies from the houseboat were sorely needed. The two doctors, father and son, set to work converting and preparing their house boat, which was now dubbed the "Angel Boat" in honor of the natives who named it, into a well-equipped floating med clinic. The porch where the gang plank entered the boat from shore would be the patient reception area, and folks and families could sit at the tables as they awaited medical attention. Food could be offered to those in need in that way as two of Dr. Armstrong's favorite tribe folk friends were soon at home in the kitchen of the boat, and they could prepare meals for needy families who came onboard. Craig saw how this would

The Case of the Skeptic Doctor

be an ideal place to begin sharing some Gospel truth with the visiting patients, knowing that salvation was the greatest need. They had brought a good supply of Bible Story Books onboard Old Gabe and had loaded them in the houseboat. In the story books were pictures of such things as the Creation, and Noah's Ark, and stories like the dividing of the Red Sea, and Gideon's 300, and the New Testament stories about Jesus and His crucifixion and resurrection. They hoped the pictures would open the minds of the poor natives and lead to discussion of the Good News of a God that loves them.

After a few days their first medical expedition was in the plans. Myko was now fully recovered except for a slight limp, and so a visit to his village was their first undertaking. It would take only two or three hours to reach the village, and so with several natives to assist them the two doctors and Bob and Arty set out to reach them.

Myko's deep affection for his new white man friends was obvious, and after a slow but steady journey through flooded swamp water, they reached the region. A crowd of natives

Reunion

stood on the shore most interested in the strange boat approaching. Some of them recognized Myko onboard, and a stir of excitement soon followed as a messenger boy ran back to the village to inform the chief...Myko's father. Soon Niko, Myko's younger brother, came running to the shore and was joyed at seeing his older, presumed lost, brother waving from the deck of the ship. The pitiful folk were half starved and so as food was offered and brought to shore, they received it with eager readiness, and some of them spoke briefly with Myko, but the language was not easily understood. Their chatter was a mystery, but Myko would interpret their words and said that they were most grateful to have some food, and that they had given up hope of ever seeing Myko again.

At last the chief arrived and Myko's mother, and they were moved with emotion upon seeing the lost son! They talked for a good while together, and Myko kept looking over at Craig and his father and Bob and Arty and with a smile pointing. Obviously the boy was speaking well of them to his father. And then the boy came and got a basket of sandwiches and brought them

The Case of the Skeptic Doctor

to his father and mother. Sitting on a woven mat the chieftain father and Myko's mother and his brother Niko all enjoyed a long conversation while the white doctors and Bob and Arty waited on their new village friends. At last Myko rose from his father's side and went to Arty and Bob and Craig and his father, and told them that his chieftain father had changed his mind about Dr. Armstrong and his friends, and said that they were good men who came to help and do good for the poor natives. Myko said that the man Paris, who had said that Dr. Armstrong was a bad man and not to be trusted, was wrong and now his father knew differently. The chieftain arose and came up to Dr. Armstrong, and with a faint smile had good words to share that Myko interpreted.

"My father says white doctor good man and says Paris not good man, because he no come to help poor natives. Paris say his great god come help natives, but no come," Myko translated his father's words into English. "My father say he give diamonds to Dr. Armstrong and no more to Paris."

Upon hearing this Dr. Armstrong replied

Reunion

shaking his head, "We seek not your diamonds but your good health and well being."

But Myko said his father would be badly offended if they didn't take the diamonds, that he held out in a pouch in his hand, that contained a good quantity of them. Dr. Armstrong knew they were low grade diamonds and not worth great sums, but they would still bring a good return in the States for covering expenses. With a warm smile the elder doctor reached out and took the gift, and Myko turning to Bob and Arty offered them a similar small pouch which the brothers wisely accepted and bowed in appreciation. Arty knew that his brother had over extended their resources when he helped to buy the river houseboat with Craig, but now they both realized how God does re-pay those who give generously and cheerfully.

Then the chieftain invited the doctors and all to come to their village for a festivity that afternoon, and they eagerly accepted the invitation hoping to promote good will between them. They were, however, glad they would be supplying a good part of the food, knowing that the natives had a taste for rather weird foods like

The Case of the Skeptic Doctor

salamanders and snakes and snails. Arty whispered to Bob, "No wonder these natives are so thin and fit! If Americans followed the salamander diet they would trim down real fast I'm sure."

Bob was amused at his brother's comment, as they continued putting together some things to take to the nearby village.

The feast in honor of the joyful reunion of Myko and his family was a good time to get acquainted with the other families in the village. As the day was ending Dr. Armstrong and his staff with Bob and Arty and Craig returned to their medical boat and slept well in their rooms onboard. The next day they would remain there and minister to health needs.

The following day, in early afternoon, the chief wanted to take them on a tour of their jungle region which included a hike to the nearby abandoned diamond pit. As they walked up to it they noted the wide roads that were once used by trucks and equipment to access the mine. It had been a number of years since the mine was operated. But as they walked around in the gravelly base of the pit, they noticed the natives keep-

Reunion

ing a keen eye for the telltale glitter of a small diamond amongst the gravel. Every once in a while a native would reach down and retrieve a tiny glittering stone and bring it to the chief and it was put in a small pouch. Most of the diamonds found were only of industrial grade, and they didn't know what a bag of them was worth, but if Paris coveted them so much, Dr. Armstrong assumed that they would give a good return in the States. Dr. Armstrong spoke to his son with disgust at his old pal Paris' scheme to gain access to the diamonds by pretending they were giving them to appease God. "Paris stirred up this chieftain against me to keep me from finding out his devices."

"Yeah, Father," Craig said, "when mother knew Paris was down here she felt pretty doubtful of his good intentions."

"Hmm..." his father reflected.

Later in the afternoon they returned to the village and went out to their medical boat. The elderly chieftain accompanied them to the boat, and gazing upon the boat the old chief smiled and said as Myko interpreted, "My son saved by river boat. Our ancestors saved many

The Case of the Skeptic Doctor

many years ago in very great boat full of animals when mighty God saved mans and animals from great flood that cover all hills." Then he raised his hands and arms above his head describing a great expanse.

Dr. Armstrong noticed the sincerity of the old chief in retelling the story of the flood as the chief had heard it, no doubt, many times, but the old man's comment reminded Bob of a picture in the Bible Story Book of Noah's Ark, and so Bob went onboard and found the boxes full of the story books that they were going to use to teach the Bible, by pictures, to the natives. As the old chieftain came onboard and sat at one of the tables there in the porch of the boat, Bob brought the book and showed the picture of Noah and his Ark to the old chief. He studied the picture with intense childlike reverence for many minutes, and then looking up muttered something in his language, and Bob looked to Myko for translation.

"My father asks if this is the story of great waters that covered all lands?"

"Yes," Bob said nodding to the chief.

Then the chief said, motioning to a chair

Reunion

at the table, "Come, sit down and tell chief story."

The old chief, like an eager child at his mother's knee, listened as Bob retold the story of the great flood with Myko translating it to his father.

Meanwhile Dr. Armstrong had come out on the deck and was listening to Bob tell the story, and noticed the descriptions the old chief was adding as he and Bob discussed the flood. This caught Dr. Armstrong's attention, and he marvelled, that here an ignorant native should have such belief in this old tale of a universal flood that was passed down to him from his ancestors. "Yet," he thought to himself, "why does he believe it, but most Americans don't want to believe it, even though the Bible gives the details of this event, and many Christian speak passionately about the truth of it? They, like me," he thought, "don't believe it because they don't want to believe it."

Bob didn't know that Dr. Armstrong was behind him listening to the discussion. But the senior doctor couldn't help but notice Bob's earnest sincerity in adding details to the story, speaking with such assurance and passion.

The Case of the Skeptic Doctor

"He obviously believes the story to be true," Armstrong thought to himself.

When Bob had finished he looked to the face of the chief and said with Myko interpreting, "Do you believe this story true?"

"Oh, yes," the chieftain replied nodding, "but never saw it, but know story be true because old fathers tell same story that old chief heard when a young boy, and old village fathers no tell lies, but speak truth."

Just then Craig came out and noticed his father standing there quietly listening to the discussion between Bob and the chief. Turning about Bob then noticed his audience and hoped he had not said anything that would put the elder doctor on the defensive.

Instead, the elder doctor could see that Bob's warm discussion with the chief was sincere, and it came from the heart, and for some reason the doctor's resistance to the age-old story was beginning to crumble as he hoped he wasn't being blindly obstinate in believing in something that did, indeed, happen.

Chapter 12

The Skeptic's Quest

For years it seemed the elder doctor had wanted with all his wit and human wisdom to prove his younger brother doctor wrong about his beliefs in Creation. But sometimes when an opponent is rendered weak and helpless, one no longer wishes to be against him, and so it was with his brother's passing...it had removed all the older brother's past hostilities to his beliefs, and rather now the older seemed to be moved with wanting to vindicate his younger brother, as he began to desire to take a deeper look at what his brother believed.

Also after only a few days of being with his father, Craig's changed life was becoming obvious, and one evening when the four men were sitting together Craig's father calmly asked

The Case of the Skeptic Doctor

with a curious gentle plea, "Craig, what has happened to you? You seem different and peaceful now, and I've noticed you reading the Bible...tell me what has happened in your life?"

Craig felt himself getting nervous, and remembering about the need to be careful not to be too aggressive said, "Well, I went to Aunt Lydia's Bible study on Creation just wanting to console her with the death of Uncle Lee, and knowing how important Creation science was to them both I was just going to go along with it when I met Bob and Arty, and they shared with me some things on Creation that got me thinking and questioning some things that I had so confidently believed all my life. And because, I thought, like you, that Creation science was shallow and easily dismissed, I was just going to politely listen to them so as not to offend them. But as they explained some things from the Creation viewpoint, I began to realize how much more logical and plausible their view point was, and so I began to question my own beliefs instead of doubting theirs...and then when I experienced some other things that the Bible talks about in my own life, I made some unexpected

The Skeptic's Quest

discoveries."

"Hmm," his father replied and seemed to want to continue the discussion, "you know I've been coming down here for several years, and I've run into tribes folks that tell a tale like the old chief did the other day, of a type of universal flood that took place ages ago that involved a big boat and how the world was judged, and only a few were delivered. And I realized these folks didn't get their ideas from the Bible, but it had passed down from generation to generation. They also tell a story of a night that lasted twice as long as normal, but I have no idea what that tale is from."

"That's interesting," Craig replied glancing to Bob for an explanation.

" The long night could have to do with the time in Joshua's day when the sun stood still about a whole day on the other side of the earth, and there are a couple hundred stories of tribesmen all over the globe telling of a great flood, that have a similar theme like that of Noah's flood, and obviously these tribal folks are not trying to validate these Bible stories, but, in fact, are validating them."

The Case of the Skeptic Doctor

"Hmm," Doctor Armstrong said contemplating, and then he asked in what seemed to be coming from a more open mind, "Bob, you and Arty are believers in Creation and I know your father is an intelligent man and believes in it, so tell me a bit more about this universal flood and what Creation scientists say about it, and why we should believe it to be true."

"Sure," Bob said gathering his thoughts and then began. "Before we talk about the flood, let's first consider what the world was like before the flood according to the Creation account in Genesis. We find in Genesis 2 that there was no rain on the earth at first, but rather there went up a 'mist from the ground and it watered the face of the whole earth,' it says."

"No rain?! I didn't know that," the older doctor said sounding surprised.

"Nope, and the Bible also says that Noah and his sons and their wives, after the flood, saw what seemed to be a new phenomena... a rainbow."

"That's interesting. I just read that, in that book on the flood my brother gave me years ago," the doctor said agreeing with Bob's comment, as Bob continued.

"There was no rainbow before the flood because there were different atmospheric conditions. Genesis Chapter One talks about 'waters above and waters below', and it implies a great body of water vapor above, not merely clouds, but a dense belt of heavy water vapor above that Creation scientists believe created an extreme 'greenhouse' atmospheric condition on the earth. This vapor canopy would have been invisible, but would have filtered out most of the cosmic and short-wave radiation that now reaches the earth. I mean just like today we know that if our atmosphere didn't filter out such radiation to a degree today, life would quickly be destroyed. But prior to the flood this canopy was much denser and thus absorbing greater amounts of radiation, and may have been part of the reason that we find men living to be as many as 7 or 8 or 9 hundred years old. Radiation causes cellular damage and genetic mutations that, in turn, cause deterioration in future generations and a decrease in vitality. And this is probably the reason that we find in Genesis, after the flood, the life span of man steadily decreasing generation after generation. This was in part brought about by the collapse of this vapor canopy."

"Interesting concept," the doctor replied seeming to be captivated with it, as Bob continued.

"This world wide 'greenhouse effect' has been verified by things like, how they have found giant mastodons with green vegetation in their stomachs frozen alive in the Arctic region. You see, this 'greenhouse effect' would have resulted in a uniform warm and subtropical climate all over the earth even in the now polar regions. At the time of the flood, God in some way caused this canopy to collapse on the earth. Then following the flood there was an abrupt freezing at the poles, because the greenhouse was removed. And so the ice age followed and gradually over maybe a thousand years receded. Days after the flood there would be, of course, a heavy run-off as the land had been 'lifted up', another phenomena recorded according to the Bible, and the ocean basins received the vast amounts of water. When we see places like the Grand Canyon, we observe the waters must have at one point been hundreds of feet deep washing out and eventually leaving the old high river terraces that we see in that canyon and canyons like it worldwide.

"Of course, that makes sense!" the doctor declared as if a light was coming on in his mind. "The flood is the only logical explanation for what we see in places like the Grand Canyon," he added with passion.

"Yes," Bob smiled and nodded and continued. "They say that with our present much thinner canopy, a worldwide rain from it would only yield about a couple of inches of water on the earth, but this canopy before the flood was much denser. And when it was caused to collapse on the earth, when it rained for 'forty days and forty nights', as the Bible says, and simultaneously with the waters coming up from the fountains of the great deep that were 'thrust up', or 'burst open' at the same time of the canopy collapse there was this surging out of a subterranean flood of water also. Every square foot of the earth's surface must have been altered and all creatures except for those at home in water, and those preserved in the Ark, must have per-

The Case of the Skeptic Doctor

ished, and many were buried alive in sediment. This rapid burying would cause the vast amount of fossils we find. As you know, Doctor, to form a fossil, something has to be mineralized quickly or it would just rot away and leave no trace of its existence."

"Exactly!" the doctor replied being captivated at the thoughts presented.

"Fossils verify that there was a rapid mineralization of these animals like the sediments from this 'thrusting up' of the earth's crust or mantel would have caused," Bob continued.

"Very interesting, and it makes so much sense," replied Dr. Armstrong who seemed to be giving over some of his past objections.

"And by the way, I might add," Bob replied, "you would think that among these millions of fossils that are found all over the world we should find numerous undisputed transitional forms of fossil examples such as animals that are part fish and part amphibian, etc., but there has never been found anywhere one example of a partly evolved creature of any kind...not one!"

"Hmmm," the doctor murmured with a subdued mind.

The Skeptic's Quest

"There is only one event in history that could account for these vast deposits of fossils, because it takes rapid burial and the shutting off of oxygen to prevent the tissues of organisms from rotting, and this with a significant mineral content in the water that would result from volcanic upheaval or thrusting up of the earth's crust, followed by a deluge of run-off stirring up this sediment to form these vast worldwide fossil deposits, deposits that are now found being left behind on dry land after God caused the waters to recede."

"That makes sense, but no transitional forms have been found, huh?" the doctor said seeming to want more reassurance.

"Not really, some animals have been found that seem to be transitional forms, but they are actually fully formed species that probably simply became extinct, like the publicized 'toothed bird' which may have been a planted hoax, or if it was a real creature it was just a toothed bird that became extinct like the dinosaurs did."

"Yeah, Dad" Craig interjected, "it was when Bob and Arty were telling me about the

The Case of the Skeptic Doctor

half ape/half man hoaxes that have been propped up over the years and taught as real in universities, where entire races of people were drawn by imaginative artists from things like one tooth and that of a tooth that was probably from an extinct pig!.. that got me to questioning what I had been so persuasively taught...and the point that if man has evolved for millions of years, then we should literally find thousands if not millions of transitional half man/half animal skeletons of fossils around all over the world, but, at best, there are only 2 or 3 that seem to be contrived, one from a strange jaw bone and another from a femur bone and a tooth. This is all rather imaginative, if not outright hoaxes, put together by those who want so much to believe their theory, when, in fact, these few rather doubtful finds are more of a verification of Creation than of Evolution."

Craig's father stared at his son realizing what he was saying was true , because as an amateur archeologist he was well aware that no good reliable missing link has ever been found.

"And you know, Craig," the father confided, "those finds of humans with small heads may not be transitional forms at all, but rather

The Skeptic's Quest

those afflicted with micro-cephalitis, a disease spread by mosquitos that is still around today!"

"Good point," Craig replied sensing his father was taking their side, so he added, "And, Father, those found with heavy brows may just be skulls of those who had lived for hundreds of years like they did before the flood, and time or years of growth, we know, causes those prominent brow features"

"Yeah, I know, that's an interesting point, too...and so the reason no reliable and true missing link has been found is simply because there aren't any," the father said conceding the obvious.

Bob nodded and said," And another interesting thing we observe when studying the fossil record at dig sites is that we see, by the order in which they were buried, a confirmation of the universal flood. For example, on the lower ground we find fish and plant fossils. We find fossilized tracks of some animals depicting them fleeing to higher ground as the flood increased. Then when they were overwhelmed in the flood, we find these larger land animals fossilized higher up. Then at the very highest ground we find fossils of some animals and people buried alive where they had tried to escape from the rising waters. You see, the fossil record gives a good picture of what that awful year of the global flood was like, and nothing in the fossil record describes anything related to Evolution. Oh, sure, we find the skeletons of extinct creatures in the fossils, but just because an animal has gone extinct it doesn't mean it was any kind of 'link' creature. We hear every year of some animal of our day going extinct, so these fossil discoveries are not evolved creatures at all but simply extinct ones, some of them being preserved on the Ark only to go extinct years later like the dinosaurs."

"Interesting, but that brings up another thing," Doctor Armstrong interjected, "I mean what you are describing makes perfect logical sense and is fascinating, but how could possibly all the species of the earth be preserved in just a big boat...and putting dinosaurs onboard, that seems impossible, too?"

Bob smiled kindly and said, "Just consider this when you think about dinosaurs on the Ark. We know reptiles keep on growing their

The Skeptic's Quest

entire life and can live for hundreds of years in the right conditions, growing larger and larger. But wouldn't Noah select a young pair of smaller dinosaurs, and smaller and younger other reptiles and mammals like elephants etc.? The younger ones would be in their prime and more hearty. And there are not that many extra large creatures anyway. It has been computed that the average sized animal would be smaller than the size of an average sheep. And as far as the size of the Ark, it was no small boat." Bob continued, "The Bible tells us the Ark was 300 cubits long, 50 cubits wide and 30 cubits tall. The exact length of the cubit is known by archeologists to be 18 to 20 inches or so. This makes the Ark around 450 feet long and 75 feet wide and 45 feet tall and was to be built in 3 tiers or levels, each level being 15 feet high or so. This ship was huge, about the size of a large ocean-going barge. There would have been about 34,000 square feet of floor space, and the smaller animals could have been put in cages and stacked on top of each other. Stalls could have been made for larger animals like elephants or dinosaurs. And being generous it is known that there are less than 20,000 land animals species living today, and if there were more in Noah's day say even 30,000, and with two of each this would give 60,000 animals, and if we compute their average size to be about the size of an average sheep, do you know how many sheep you could fit in a ship this size...about 140,000! So, you see, even with being generous with the number of animals onboard, it would still only occupy less than half the Ark's capacity, thus giving plenty of room for food and fresh water," Bob said pausing.

"I'm probably like most people who have never stopped to think about how large that ship was," Doctor Armstrong admitted yielding up again his doubtful objections. Then looking to his son he said,"Craig, are you beginning to believe all of this that the Bible says is true?"

Craig was realizing that as a Christian one always faces the risk of alienating a close friend or relative by speaking the truth, but love at times compels us to do so, so he tactfully answered, "I was becoming more open to it after talking with Bob and Arty one evening after Aunt Lydia's Creation Bible study when they explained the missing link hoaxes. But it was when I experienced in my own life one of the miracles that the Bible talks about, that I became convinced that the other miracles in the Bible were probably true, too, and even the Creation account."

"Huh," his father replied in a searching tone of voice, "what was that? Tell me about it."

"Well, Jesus speaks of being 'born again' or 'born of the Spirit', and there are other places in the New Testament that talk about becoming a new creation in Christ. The Bible talks about being renewed by the Spirit of God the moment we surrender and put our full trust in Jesus to save us. And so one night when I was feeling particularly disappointed in myself, and felt as if most of my life I had only given God my duty instead of my heart, I prayed a simple prayer of faith and called out for Christ to forgive my sins and come into my life and be my Lord and Savior. At that instant I felt this amazing 'renewing' that the Bible talks about in my own life. After that prayer I felt so peaceful and different for the first time. The next day I had love for others, a joy, and peace in my heart, and I knew

The Case of the Skeptic Doctor

Christ was with me in Spirit. It's hard to explain, Dad," Craig said. "But, I knew I was for the first time a friend of God, and this was not just a passing emotional experience, but it was real and I have felt this closeness with God ever since that night. I wasn't pretending or trying to just work up these feelings either, and then I began to see other places in the Bible where men had come to a personal experience in knowing God through faith in His Son, Jesus, and I knew exactly what had happened in their lives. I had made fun of those who claimed to be 'born again' most of my adult life, but all of a sudden I realized I had been wrong. And so I thought if this incredible miracle of coming to know God was true, and to be experienced, then I realized that all those miracles about Creation and the flood and the dividing of the Red Sea, and the walls of Jericho falling down, and many others that I used to scoff at, were probably real, too." Craig said.

His father looked up and studied the faces of the three young men, and then in kindness and deep thoughtfulness said, "This is giving me a lot to think about, boys. I can tell you're sincere, and it isn't some religious idea you're trying to convince yourselves of either."

"No, Father, it's not religion I'm trying to follow," Craig replied. "It's a relationship I have with God's Son, and it's God who is keeping me faithful to Himself. It's not me working at it."

"Hmm," the elder doctor replied, "I see that, but it's getting late now and thanks for not being afraid to share this with me, fellas...I can tell it's coming from your hearts, and I'm going to be thinking about these things."

It had been a good day, but Bob and Arty and Craig knew it would take more than convincing facts and personal testimonies to change the heart of the skeptic doctor. It would take prayer and the power of God, and so they kept praying he would seek and hopefully find.

Chapter 13

The Skeptic Wrestles

Where there is a seeking heart, there is a loving God helping those who seek to find. Craig and the Baxter brothers kept praying for the doctor's spiritual needs, and Craig noticed one day while in his father's thatch-roofed cottage, that he had the book on the flood his brother had given him years before turned face down where he had left off reading on the endtable next to his recliner. This was a good sign, but little did they know the intense struggle that was going on in the elder doctor's mind. The answers he had gotten concerning the flood and Creation were obviously easier and more logical to accept and believe than all the theories of Evolution he had once held so dearly and had so obstinately believed in. It was now obvious in

The Case of the Skeptic Doctor

his mind that the theories surrounding Evolution were basically beliefs that were founded on rather unsupported science, and so he was now at a point where he dared not to ask any more questions. It was no longer a matter of being convinced, it was a matter of being willing. Furthermore, his own son's changed life was obvious, and the father knew he wasn't just acting it out. But was he willing to make a similar commitment to Christ? This was the thought he was wrestling with. Then a few days later Craig noticed a Bible on the endtable alongside the book on the flood. He mentioned this to Bob and Arty, and Bob's reply was, "That's good! The Word of God is powerful in converting the soul."

But these were busy days for the medical supply boat team, as they visited stranded villages and distributed their storehouse of food that was onboard. But it didn't take long for their stock to be depleted, and so Bob and Arty and Craig made plans to go back to Mauaus and re-supply the ship.

Craig's father had a handful of letters that he wished his son to send home to his wife and friends at the Boston med clinic, and, of course,

The Skeptic Wrestles

he wanted them to get his mail at the post office in Manaus and bring it back. So they left early Monday morning and set out on a steady course, and now that the rains were subsiding and a dry spell seemed to be in the offing they made good progress.

Upon arriving in Manaus they decided to split up, and Bob and Craig would go to the markets and buy and stow onboard the ship all the food and goods the ship could hold. Arty set out for the post office and then to check on their plane and get a few things from off it. One thing he was going to get was the box of shotgun shells he had left onboard the plane. He wasn't expecting any more jungle safari action, but in any event he wanted to have more than just a pocketful of ammunition just in case.

At the post office Arty mailed the letters to the States, and was given by the clerk a stack of letters for the senior doctor, among which he noticed one from Rochester, NY, with the return address of 'Bill Paris' on it. Later that afternoon the trio met back at dockside and were ready for the return voyage in the morning.

Arty gave the letters to Craig, and along

with a couple of letters from his mother to his dad he noticed the one from Bill Paris and announced his name to Bob and Arty with a tone of disdain in his voice. "Dad said to go ahead and read any letters that I might need to respond to and mail them back a letter or note before returning," Craig said opening the letter from Paris. "I feel like writing a note back to Bill Paris and telling him to just stay put in Rochester," Craig said as he skimmed over it. But then said, "Oh, good, looks like Paris won't be coming back down until August! He says he's getting an extensive overhaul of the plane's engine done there in Rochester."

"Must still have plenty of gems to last a while," Bob muttered.

"This is another thing we need to be praying about, I mean that my father wouldn't be so gullible in allowing Paris to come back down here! I'm afraid he's just going to stir up trouble," was Craig's sober assessment.

"Whenever the Lord's doing a good work, the enemy usually comes along and tries to cause trouble...so let's be praying something will intervene," Arty proposed.

The Skeptic Wrestles

"What do you guys think about me writing a note to Paris and telling him that he's not needed down here anymore," Craig wondered.

"You could," Bob said thinking, "but it would be taking matters into your own hands, and wouldn't you rather see how the Lord can handle it and protect you and your father?"

"Yeah, good point, you're right! I know it's best to leave it in God's hands, but I'm tempted, too," Craig said holding back his words knowing Bob was right.

The next morning they refueled the boat and set out for the medical clinic compound and reached it in two days without any incident, and Craig's father seemed to be in up-beat spirits and happy for their safe return. Going through his mail at lunch he was eager to read the latest letter from his wife. He smiled as he finished it and then handing it to Craig said, "I think you'll find this interesting! You might want to read it later."

"Oh," Craig said putting the letter in his shirt pocket.

Then his father commented on the letter from Bill Paris, "Sound's like Bill's coming down in August."

"Yeah, we know," Craig answered. "I read his letter in case we needed to reply to him for you," he said looking over to the brothers.

Later that evening while the fellas were in their bunk room on the boat Craig pulled the letter from his mom out and was reading it. "You guys will hardly believe this," Craig said glancing up from the letter with a broad smile. "My mom says she's been reading through the Gospels and enjoying going to lunch one day a week with Jen and finding her gentle comments about the Lord most uplifting. Mom says it's the high light of her week going to lunch and talking with Jen about God. Mom says Jen's so uplifting...isn't this interesting?" Craig commented looking up to Bob and Arty with a smile! "My mom doesn't realize how much she is encouraging my dad with this letter."

"And you didn't think you said enough to your mom back before we left. Your comment about how you had been reading the Bible probably really spoke to her, Craig," Bob replied.

"And she could probably sense your new deeper peace and changed life," Arty added.

The Skeptic Wrestles

"Well," Craig said laying aside the letter, "I guess we need to be praying more for my mom, too...it seems like the Lord's working in the hearts of both of my parents."

In the next few weeks of May the team was thankful the rains had at last subsided for the most part, and the flood waters were receding. They had been busy assisting stranded natives and going around to the villages, and some places where the houses were built on stilts, they knew their food supplies had to be very scanty if they had any food at all other than fish.

Coming up to one of those villages built out over the water Dr. Armstrong pointed as Craig maneuvered their ship towards the houses.

"That's a relief," Dr. Armstrong said pointing to one of the nearby thatch houses. "I flew over here to survey the flood damage back before my runway was under water, and the flood water was all the way up to the doorway of these houses here."

Craig maneuvered the houseboat closer when just then a poor native lady with a baby in her arms came to the doorway. Dr. Armstrong was out on the front of the boat and waved.

The Case of the Skeptic Doctor

"That's a relief," Dr. Armstrong said pointing to one of the nearby thatch houses, "I flew over here to survey the flood damage back before my runway was under water, and the flood water was all the way up to the doorway of these houses here."

The Skeptic Wrestles

He was familiar to these folks and was always welcome! He had helped them a great deal with his medical services. The lady smiled and waved back and then disappeared from the doorway and seconds later was back accompanied with her husband and a few older children all waving and smiling.

The senior doctor with the help of some of his native staff were now talking with the family and, as they carefully moved alongside with the boat they were able to reach out some food supplies to the father. He was gaunt and thin but smiled and called out something in appreciation as he took the packages.

For the next few days they were busy with similar efforts to distribute food and supplies to various tribal folk, and finally they returned to their own compound. The next couple of weeks the flood waters steadily declined, and the doctor estimated that in another month's time their landing strip would be open and maybe even able to be used.

But for some reason that Craig couldn't understand he noticed his father had become more silent and sullen of late, and the Bible was

The Case of the Skeptic Doctor

no longer out on the endtable. Craig was worried that maybe he had offended him by being so cheery and positive about life, or maybe it was the Bible and Creation discussions, that his father had actually initiated and wanted at breakfast a few mornings, that had upset the elder doctor, and so Craig took his concern to Bob and Arty one night.

"Oh, don't worry about your dad," Arty said, "he's probably just under conviction. It may be a good sign that the Holy Spirit is doing His work of convicting...it's not easy to yield up the will to God."

"Especially when you have been so sure all your life that Christians are just narrow-minded simpletons and do-gooders," Craig replied sighing.

"Right," added Bob, "and Christians aren't perfect either, and we're subject to the same temptations and shortcomings as anyone else! We're just forgiven."

"A couple of verses come to my mind," Arty commented pausing from the gentle hymn he was strumming on his guitar, "one says something like, 'in the day of salvation I have helped thee,' and another says 'He who has begun a good work in you will continue to perform it until the day of Christ'."

"Those are good verses," Craig said feeling more hopeful.

"And remember, Craig," Bob said, " salvation is a gift of God, not of works, the Bible says...not your father's works, or our works in trying to convince him. We've said enough for now. Let's just be praying and let God do His work in your father's heart."

"Okay, thanks, guys, I guess I was just needing some reassurance."

The next day to their surprise Myko arrived at their compound in a canoe. They hadn't seen him for over a month. He was looking for Craig and Arty and said that his father had sent him to ask if Craig and his friends could come and teach more from picture book of God."

Craig smiled at the invitation and when he related the event to his father, Dr. Armstrong was a little concerned because he knew he had a couple of surgeries coming up, and he would like his son's assistance. So instead it was decided to send Arty alone with Myko. But before they

The Case of the Skeptic Doctor

left, Myko asked Arty if he could bring along big "boom gun" with him.

"Sure, Myko," Arty smiled, "that's been kinda handy for us, hasn't it...I wondered why I grabbed that box of shells?" Arty added looking over to get his brother's reaction.

"Not this time...I've got a better idea," Bob protested. "How about we taking you back to Myko's place in the Angel Boat, and then maybe you won't need those shells!"

"You're spoiling all my fun," Arty grinned. "But I'm all for it," he added sounding relieved.

"One of our surgeries is over that way," the senior doctor stated. "Maybe we can drop Arty off and then go do that surgery; it's on a man who has a large growth I've got to remove...hopefully it's benign."

Later that afternoon they headed over to Myko's village, but found with the receded flood waters that they had to anchor a ways off and ferry the supplies and a box of story books over by means of Myko's canoe. Arty would stay there a few days and try to teach the open hearted natives about God and the miracles God can do.

The Skeptic Wrestles

Arty was encouraged with the way it worked out for him to get closer to Myko and his brother Niko and father and mother, and try to help them with spiritual things. Arty took along his guitar that all the villagers greatly enjoyed hearing.

The Angel Boat went about delivering food and supplies, and the doctors were able to perform the surgeries that needed their attention and to help some other sick folks. At last they returned to the Armstrong compound, and then Bob and Craig set sail once again for Manaus to stock up the ship with supplies.

What seemed destined to be an uneventful trip to Manaus ended up being a most joyous occasion as Craig had gotten a letter from his mother telling how she had found Christ, and now knew that same peace that she saw in her son's life.

"I can hardly believe it!" he said to Bob after sharing the good news with him. "She says she's going to be praying for dad and us that we will help him find Jesus!"

She had written a long letter to her husband, and when he read it at dinner the evening Bob and Craig returned from Manaus, he looked

The Case of the Skeptic Doctor

up from the letter, and stared over his glasses, smiled, and said to Bob and Craig, "Looks like I'm surrounded by a bunch of religious fanatics! But, but," he grinned, " I'm beginning to wonder if there isn't something to it! You couldn't all be pretending."

Chapter 14

The Skeptic Surrenders

In the next few weeks as the doctor wrestled with the fate of his own life, he had many inward questions. If it was a matter of simply giving mental assent to the facts of Creation and the flood, the doctor had convincing proofs that they were true events. He even knew that the experience of the new birth in Christ had to be real...why would those so dear to him be simply making up a story about this if they hadn't experienced it? They would gain nothing by simply fabricating it. And the peace and faith they displayed was proof enough something was real about it. So the doctor confessed to Craig that he believed it was all true, but didn't know what he should do at this point in his own life. Craig meekly suggested he try reading the New Testa-

The Case of the skeptic Doctor

ment with a meditative and open mind to the message it contained. The elder doctor agreed to this, and slowly day after day he worked his way through the Gospels.

Craig was growing to be at home with the native people. His heart went out to them in their deep need for the God who loved them. Craig had visited Arty at Myko's village, and saw the way he simply told the Bible stories from the pictures in the story books; Craig decided to return to his father's compound and do the same. He soon had a class of eager learners.

Bob kept busy with some native men working on the landing strip which was now free of flood water, but was covered with logs, silt, vines and other debris that had floated out from the surrounding jungle. A week later Bob and Craig took the Angel Boat over to pick up Arty. Arty found it difficult to pull himself away from his new friends, some of whom had professed faith in Christ. Craig would have to take over in ministering to them in a few weeks.

The elder doctor had continued his search to be at peace with God, and having noticed Bob and Arty and Craig taking walks to meditate and

The Skeptic Surrenders

pray on the trails in the wooded areas around their compound, decided to do the same. His inner struggles continued, however, and he was about to give up on his quest when one afternoon, after a brief rain shower, the elder doctor grabbed his New Testament and went out for a walk. He came to a familiar spot along the trail where there was a log to sit upon, and turning to the place where he had left off (he had come to the story of the rich young ruler in Luke chapter 18), he was intrigued by the story of this well-to-do young man. "Here was a story of one who had everything yet was still seeking," the doctor thought to himself of the verse he just read, 'What shall I do to inherit eternal life?' the young man had asked Jesus...the One who knew."

He had read the story before in the other two Gospels, but for some reason it was standing out to him now. He noticed the first thing that Jesus said to the rich young ruler was that "None is good, except one, and that is God."

"I wonder if this young man thought he was good?" the doctor reflected looking up from the page and gazing into the jungle. Then he noticed how Jesus told him to keep the com-

The Case of the Skeptic Doctor

mandments like "do not kill, do not steal...honor mother and father". But the young man replies to Jesus, "All these I have kept from my youth."

The doctor sat contemplating, and recalling his own youth as he thought to himself, "Sounds a lot like me...I could always keep the commandments the rules around the house when Lee and I were growing up. Mom would say don't do this or that, and I would always obey! It was Lee who would usually disobey, and he was the socializing kind, too, in college, and I kept away from that, and just studied and stayed out of trouble! It was Lee who was the mischievious one, not me," the doctor reasoned to himself. He reflected upon how Lee and his wife lived in a nice big comfortable home. "But it was me who gave all that up and came down here to live this primitive self-sacrificing life.....How did my brother Lee suddenly become the good one?" the older brother thought to himself feeling a little perturbed.

"Hmm," he read on, "Jesus said sell all and give to the poor...well, that's what I've done! I've given up all the riches I could have had for these poor natives...I don't understand it!" He

The Skeptic Surrenders

sat there feeling annoyed. "What more could I have done?" He read on.

"Sell all...and come and follow me," Jesus says. "Yeah, I guess it's true. Lee tried to follow Jesus, in spite of the ridicule and mocking he knew he would get from all our intellectual friends...he gave up or sold his fair reputation among them...but I suppose I have come down here to look noble to my peers...not to sell but to gain a good reputation...hmm," he thought, as he began to see through his own facade. "Yeah, I have a pride, that's it. A secret pride in my own goodness, in giving up my good life, and in all of this I'm doing down here to look humble and good." Suddenly he was beginning to sense his own self-righteous pride. "Pride, he smirked, "in my own good deeds." His thoughts were revealing a side of his life he had not ever seen or wanted to see.

While the doctor sat pondering he heard a commotion in the nearby trees, and so he stood up and came to his feet and crept slowly towards the noise...it sounded like children's voices, and then he saw a couple of young native lads playing. They had a wooden box with a small rope

The Case of the Skeptic Doctor

tied to it and a hole bored in the box. It was clear to Armstrong what the boys were doing, they were trying to catch a monkey. It was an old trick that the children often used to catch them, and monkeys could be sold to tourists in the markets in towns like Manaus for a fairly good price. The trick was to fascinate the monkey climbing there in the nearby trees with a bright white pebble that they would put in the hole in the wooden box, and then they would tip the box up and shake the pebble out to make the monkey curious about it and want the white pebble. So the boys dropped the white pebble in the box. As the monkey watched on, they set the box out for the curious little monkey, and then the boys slipped away into the foliage, and hid themselves holding on to the rope attached to the box.

The doctor watched on with a smile as the ruse continued; and, sure enough, after a few moments the curious monkey climbed down from his perch above and proceeded with caution to the box, and squeezing his paw through the hole in the box, and reaching in and feeling for the stone, he at last grasped it in his paw.

The Skeptic Surrenders

But now with the stone in his hand, there was not room enough in the small hole in the box to withdraw his paw while holding the stone in his grasp at the same time. He would have to drop the pebble to get his hand out, and, of course, he was not willing to do that. So the monkey was trapped by his own unwillingness to let go of the pebble, and the doctor watched as the boys slowly drew the box towards them with the rope; and once the monkey was within reach, they would spring upon him and catch him. At last the frustrated monkey who was unwilling to let go of his treasure was within the grasp of the boys, and they seizing him gave a shout of triumph as they grabbed the monkey by the back of the neck because they knew he would try to bite them. But once caught they would soon train the animal with gentle patting and snacks that they would not harm him, and in time, he would grow tame. Seconds later the lads raced off to the village eager to show their friends their catch, and Dr. Armstrong returned to his place upon the log and sat pondering what all of this was about.

"What am I unwilling to let go of to give

The Case of the Skeptic Doctor

up to follow Jesus? It says this young ruler went away sad because he would not give up his riches...and I, too, am sad, what are the riches I will not give up? But I've given over my riches, haven't I? I've sacrificed a lot to come down here to the jungles and give myself for these people. I've given up having a nice fancy house, and prestigious practice! As he sat there thinking he suddenly realized the game he had been playing with himself and others, and even with God. "But this has been done to glorify my own name, of course it is...I've been trying to show how good I am in giving up my wealth and living sacrificially, but most of it has been doing it for nothing more than to try to look better than others...especially my brother Lee. I've been trying to look like the 'good' self-sacrificing doctor, but the root of it is pride of being spoken and thought well of, just like I did growing up always trying to look better than Lee, and others I knew were into dubious things. How much I relished being thought of as a 'good boy', and I'm still playing that game now. That's what I'm holding on to, that's my pebble...my own goodness and fair reputation, I've trapped my-

The Skeptic Surrenders

self and will not let go of feeling I'm the 'good doctor'! From my youth I was always told how good a boy I was, and I've kept up the show of this all these years."

Suddenly Jesus' words seemed to resound in his mind..."None is good, except one, and that is God."

"That's the very first thing Jesus said to this young ruler...as if it was the first thing He wanted him to realize!" The thoughts struck deep, and he felt guilty and in need of forgiveness.

"I've lived to be good, and this is my riches, and part of it is also being right about things like Evolution and thinking Christians are simpletons for believing in the flood and Creation and the Bible, in general. But I've deceived myself just like this rich young ruler, and look how easily Jesus saw right into his heart and tried to get him to see that he wasn't good at all, and, in fact, he was in love with his own goodness and riches far more than he loved the Son of God. This is my problem! It's my heart! I love my goodness, my smartness, my sacrificial living, my Evolution religion, and all of this is my little

The Case of the Skeptic Doctor

pebble that I will not let go of."

It was at that very moment that his heart was laid openly bare in front of his eyes, and he was smitten as vile before God. He sat there a while ashamed of his own pride, until at last he turned, and got down on his knees, and with hands folded and elbows on the log, he begged the Lord to forgive his pride and all his other sins, and his stubbornness in not being willing to yield to the Lordship of Christ. He, then and there, in a simple but believing prayer of surrender, yielded up all his pride, confessed that he was a sinner, and then after a good long while he rose up following Jesus with all his heart. His quest was over!

It didn't take but a few days for Bob and Arty and Craig to notice his changed life. And then the doctor himself was sharing the humorous story of how he saw himself on that fateful walk on the jungle trail as nothing more than a curious little monkey who thought he was good and smart.

"And you know," the doctor said at dinner, "I believe in Creation now, because I feel so new! I know I'm a new creation now in

The Skeptic Surrenders

Christ...isn't there a verse that says something like that?"

"Yes, there is, Father," Craig replied. "I think it's in 2nd Corinthians 5 ...it says 'if any man be in Christ he's a knew creature or a new creation, old things have passed away, behold, all things have become new.'"

The older doctor smiled at the thought of it. And now joy had taken the place of heaviness in his life, and in the days that followed he began writing a letter to his wife telling of his new found faith in Christ, and there was great joy at the compound.

A few weeks passed, and then one morning at breakfast the elder doctor said, "Craig, do you think you could fly our Beechcraft down here from New York?"

"Sure, Father, I suppose...I might need a few lessons from Bob and Arty first," he said looking up to his friends.

"Sure, Craig, we could fly over to Rochester and spend some time with you giving some flight lessons," Bob proposed.

"Good," said the older doctor and then continued, "I wonder, Craig if you would mind

The Case of the Skeptic Doctor

delivering this letter to Bill Paris. He's over in Rochester. I wrote to him telling him I didn't need his help down here anymore, and that I would suggest that he refrain from his questionable activities at the diamond mine with those natives, and I know this may not prevent him from coming back down here, but at least I don't need to supply his transportation." The doctor smiled and went on, "And I included a lengthy discussion on how I have found the Lord Jesus, and I recommended Him to Bill, and I hope he will heed my admonitions, and Craig," his father continued, "I'm wondering if you would mind flying down and picking me up in a few weeks. I've got to stay around and attend to some medical needs but..." and then Craig interjected.

"Dad, I was wondering if it would upset you if I quit school and joined you down here as your assistant and intern?"

"Are you serious...I mean I was going to suggest that, but I know how important those medical degrees are," the father replied.

"Dad, there was a time when being called 'doctor' was important to me, but it doesn't matter anymore, and besides the natives call me

The Skeptic Surrenders

'little doc' anyway, and that's enough," he grinned.

The flight back to the States in Old Gabe was filled with joy at the wonderful work the Lord had done. Bob and Arty with Craig returned to Vermont to report to their family the great work the Lord had done on their mission. Old Grandma and Grandpa Baxter rejoiced to hear how their prayers were answered and how the Lord used the things they had given them. Craig got his car and went home to visit his mom and stay for a few days, and then he went over to Rochester, New York, to see about his father's plane. Then Bob and Arty flew over to Rochester and spent a couple weeks flying with Craig everyday as he honed in his flying skills. Satisfied that the young doctor was well able to fly to South America to be with his father, Bob and Arty went back to Vermont to wait to hear from the Lord about their next assignment.

Then one day a few weeks later Bob and Arty received a letter in the mail from Craig Armstrong with a return address of Boston on it.

Bob related to Arty the letter's content,

"Craig says he's on his way down to his father's compound, but before he flies down he was going to stop by his Aunt's house in Ticonderoga and say good-bye to her, and he said he wondered if we and our family would want to come over for another session of Mr. Hamilton's Creation Bible study. And, get this," Bob said with a big grin, "Craig says he also wants us all to meet his mother who was coming with him, and his new medical mission's assistant who is also his new bride named Jen!"

"Well, well, it sounds to me like the Lord is still in the Creation business, creating new creatures in Christ, and new families to serve Him!" Arty said with a warm smile.

The End